A Wary Welcome

The History of U.S. Attitudes Toward Immigration

Joanna Michal Hoyt

A Wary Welcome: The History of U.S. Attitudes Toward Immigration

Publisher Contact

Skinny Bottle Publishing

books@skinnybottle.com

Introduction

Immigration is one of the most important, and most deeply divisive, issues in U.S. politics today. Our current president has been elected (by less than half of the popular vote) partly on the strength of his promise to drastically curb immigration and deport undocumented immigrants. His energetic attempts to fulfill that promise have been praised by many of his supporters, condemned and resisted by other Americans. Immigration policy is debated in the federal courts, as the President's attempt to ban refugees and other travelers are challenged. It is debated at Immigration and Customs Enforcement (ICE) Centers, where undocumented immigrants who have lived here for many years, borne citizen children and become deeply embedded in their communities, go to detention hearings accompanied by neighbors, clergy, and activists pleading against their deportation. It is debated on the streets, as demonstrators mobilize against the President's counter-immigration actions and counter-protesters mobilize against the demonstrators. It is debated in newspapers, on television, from pulpits and in living rooms.

Often the debate sounds more like a shouting match than a dialogue, as each side states its case more and more loudly. The two sides characterize immigrants in different ways. Some describe legally recognized refugees and undocumented asylum seekers as families fleeing violence or starvation, in need of a safe haven and ready to share their gifts of skill, character, courage and cultural perspective with the country which gives them refuge. Others describe them as alien hordes who do not understand our culture or our values, who are likely to become public charges at the expense of already-struggling native-born citizens and who include large numbers of criminals and terrorists.

Both sides claim that they seek to protect American values but there is little agreement as to what these values are. Some describe the U.S. as a nation of immigrants and of principles; a nation profoundly committed to human rights. Others describe the U.S. as a nation of people of European descent and of laws; a nation profoundly committed to the preservation of its traditional institutions. An outside observer could be forgiven for thinking that the different sides are describing different countries.

This division is not new, nor are the basic arguments on either side.

American history rings with passionate disputes about the importance of race; about the role of immigration in economic development and the struggle for workers' rights; about national loyalty and national security in wartime; about our religious obligations to refugees, immigrants and citizens and about the fundamental nature of our country and our values.

This book is my attempt to trace the great questions about immigration back to the early days of the United States and to understand how we came to this fraught and divided state.

This attempt is complicated by the multiplicity of our narratives around immigration. There are many stories — woven through each other, cutting across each other and contradicting each other.

This multiplicity is partly based on the diversity of voluntary immigrants.[1] People came to the U.S. from across the Atlantic, across the Pacific and across the Rio Grande. They came from Latin America, from Europe, from Asia and from Africa. They came fleeing wars, fleeing pogroms, fleeing political crackdowns and fleeing starvation. They came seeking their fortunes, seeking religious freedom and seeking open land which could

---

[1] I am speaking now, as this book will speak, of those who came to the U.S. voluntarily. I do not forget that many thousands were brought against their will, chained in the holds of slave ships. America's great original sins, race-based chattel slavery and the genocide of First Nations, are painfully relevant to the questions of race, solidarity and justice which also affect the debate over voluntary immigration. They are not, however, the focus of this book; I leave them in the hands of more knowledgeable historians.

support their varied dreams. Each of these migrant groups and each individual in these groups has a different story.

The historian's task is equally complicated by the different stories which native-born, or long-naturalized, Americans have told themselves about each wave of immigrants. In the nineteenth and twenty-first centuries, Americans have disagreed, not only about what should happen but about what actually is happening. Are immigrants draining or supporting the U.S. economy? Are immigrants more or less likely than native-born citizens to commit serious crimes? Does immigration strengthen or weaken American values? Opposing answers are given and copious quantities of anecdotal and statistical evidence are used to back both sides of the argument. Some citizens struggle with what to believe. Most readily believe either one side or the other.

Our beliefs are influenced in part by what we read and where we get both our news and our history. (This fact should leave historians and journalists with a deep sense of the profound consequences of our writing.) But our convictions are as much visceral as intellectual. We are inclined to believe the stories and the studies which resonate with our own early experiences.

This is certainly true in my case. I cannot claim to be objective about immigration and immigrants. I don't know an American who is objective on this point.[2] The best I can do is to explicitly own my perspective and the experiences that have shaped me so that readers can understand my likely biases — and perhaps also consider their own.

---

[2] I do know some U.S. commentators who say that we must be objective about immigration and set aside sentimentality. Most of them object to heart-rending stories about the difficulties of the immigrant experience — but are quite willing to raise visceral fears about what the presence of strangers may do to our children, and to tell emotional stories about crimes committed by "aliens."

Most of my ancestors came into this country when it was still a British colony with unrestricted immigration. They were German, French, Irish and English — all so long ago that no stories and traditions from the old countries remain. As a child, I envied my friends whose grandparents had immigrated from Italy, who learned Italian from their relatives and got to go and visit cousins across the ocean.

As a teenager, I volunteered with my family teaching English to Sudanese and Somali kids between four and eight years old. I heard them reminisce about what they missed — friends left behind and fresh mangoes not priced so high that poor folks couldn't afford them. I also heard them speak matter-of-factly about hunger, snipers and land mines. I knew a few of their parents, people with formal manners, British accents and tired eyes; people trying to learn a new language and culture, while working long hours to support their kids and send money back home to get relatives out of camps where hunger and land mines were still part of everyday life. When politicians argue about how and whether to admit refugees, I think of them.

As a young woman, I was part of a church group working with migrant laborers who had been injured on commercial farms in the area. We never asked about their legal status. We listened to whatever they chose to tell us. Some had come here fleeing either political persecution or gang violence; more had come trying to earn enough money so their kids at home could have enough to eat and shoes so they could go to school. Some of the people talked about coming through officially sanctioned labor programs, being promised good pay and good working conditions but often getting something quite different. Others talked about crossing the desert, trying to avoid the Border Patrol and the rattlesnakes. They talked about the backbreaking work they did — work which native-born Americans depend on and often refuse to do. They talked about homesickness. They talked about being harassed by people either afraid or contemptuous of "foreigners" (even though some of the workers were Puerto Ricans, and therefore, U.S. citizens.) When public figures argue about Hispanic immigrants, I remember those men's faces.

I live and work at a nonprofit organization where we grow food to share with a local soup kitchen and invite neighbors in to learn to make and grow more for themselves. We've been helped in the work by international volunteers — from Korea, from Japan, from the Netherlands and also by a young woman from Bangladesh who worked with us during Ramadan. She was fasting, going without water as well as food and we tried to get her to rest in the shade. She kept on working and when we persisted, laughed and said, "Am I not amazing?" During the rest time, she talked about her plan to get a degree in public health and then return home and do nonprofit work. She understood both the education and the public service to be part of what her faith required of her. When public figures debate whether Muslim immigrants are dangerous, I think of her.

A Note on Language

The immigration debate is so polarized and confusing that we don't all have a common language. A word here about one point of clarity and one point of controversy:

A refugee, according to Merriam-Webster's dictionary, is, "a person seeking refuge or asylum." But in U.S. law and in the U.S. immigration debate, "refugee" refers specifically to a person whose need for refuge has been confirmed by an international body. A refugee resettlement program in America is set up specifically to serve those refugees who have been exhaustively vetted and allowed into the country by the State Department. There are others in this country who also seek refuge but who have not gone through this legal process. In this book, I will refer to such people as "asylum seekers."

There is much dispute over the correct way of referring to asylum seekers and others who enter the U.S. without first obtaining legal permission or who enter legally and overstay their visas. Those groups most hostile to such immigrants refer to them as "illegal immigrants," "illegal aliens" or just "illegals." I hold, along with many mainstream news organizations, that "illegal" is neither a noun nor an appropriate designation for such a person. In this book, I refer to such people as "undocumented immigrants." I do, however, speak of illegal immigration, since the phenomenon of crossing borders without legal papers is well-documented. Unlawful entry and visa overstaying are, at this time, civil offenses rather than crimes.

Chapter One

Mother of Exiles: The Atlantic Migration

When the United States gained independence, immigrants from Europe had been crossing the Atlantic for more than 150 years — long enough for the descendants of the first immigrants to regard themselves as long-established and quite distinct from new arrivals. The attitude of the first American leaders toward newcomers from Europe seems to have been mixed. President Washington wrote to a group of Irish immigrants that "the bosom of America is open to receive not only the opulent and respectable stranger but the oppressed and persecuted of all nations." He also wrote to an English friend that, "I have no intention to invite immigrants, even if there are no restrictive acts against it. I am opposed altogether."[i] But at this time, immigration was largely controlled by individual states — or more often — not controlled at all. The relatively small numbers of immigrants in the early period and their wide dispersal made it easy to set the question aside for later.

John Adams, Washington's successor, took a warier view of immigrants, as did the Federalist Party under his leadership. One Federalist in Congress said it was both unnecessary and unwise to "invite hordes of Wild Irishmen, nor the turbulent and disorderly of all the world, to come here with a basic view to distract our tranquility."[ii] It is difficult to say whether his concern was prompted by the fear of violence or by the fact that non-English voters had thrown their support to the Federalists' chief opponents, the Democratic-Republicans, in 1796.

The Federalists did not move to suppress immigration as such. They did, however, pass the Alien Acts. One of these allowed the President, in the event of war, to detain or deport all male citizens of that country over 14 years old who were in the U.S. when war was declared. The other act allowed him to imprison or deport any non-naturalized immigrant whom he considered, for any reason, to be "dangerous to the peace and safety of the United States." These acts were passed together with the Sedition Act, which severely limited political dissent. The whole package generated outrage across the country; the Sedition Act was repealed and the Alien Acts were quietly allowed to expire.

After Adams' time, immigration was still dealt with by states or not at all. The first attempts to organize the reception of immigrants were designed partly to protect them from exploitation. The Castle Garden Center in New York Harbor, (established in 1855), offered immigrants a place to change their money at honest rates, make contact with employers (unless they had come already under contract to a particular employer) and be referred to reputable boardinghouses that would neither grossly overcharge the men nor try to dupe the women into prostitution — all abuses which commonly happened. At first, Castle Garden offered some protection. Thirty years later, investigative journalists reported that the same abuses were now taking place within the walls of Castle Garden.

Castle Garden and later. Ellis Island, were built within view of the Statue of Liberty, hailed in her dedicatory poem as the "Mother of Exiles," whose pedestal bears the inscription still commonly quoted by immigration advocates today: "Give me your tired, your poor, your huddled masses yearning to breathe free, the wretched refuse of your teeming shore ..." This appears always to have been poetry rather than governing philosophy. The first laws governing European immigration ensured that not only criminals but also people who were sick or otherwise likely to become public charges were turned away. Those who became unable to support themselves within their first three years in the States could be, and often were, deported. Records show many such refusals and deportations, including a woman with a hunched back who was denied entry despite her pleas that she was still capable of and accustomed to hard work, and a family deported after two years in the U.S. because the father had fallen into a depression after the death of his young son and had lost his job.

Who were these immigrants who crossed the Atlantic? They came from more countries than this book has room to recount. Here are a few of the larger groups:

Irish and German immigrants arrived in large numbers in the early to mid-1800s. From the 1600s through the early 1800s, there were two distinct flows of German-American immigrants: Those who came primarily for economic reasons and those who came seeking religious liberty when religions other than Lutheranism and Catholicism were disallowed back home. Many of the latter moved into hitherto unsettled land and started communities with shared religious bonds; some of these were communes with utopian visions. The communes tended to fail but the immigrants remained, and in many cases, prospered. German-Americans had a propensity to arrive in full family groups.

In the early years, Irish-Americans more often arrived singly; the first wage-earner in a family established him- or herself and then sent passage money for relatives. Some Irish immigrants left their country because of poverty; others fled the political crackdown that followed the 1798 uprising against England.

The 1845 potato famine hit both Ireland and Germany hard. Families who had been poor but coping, were suddenly starving. Many took passage to America. These immigrants could barely afford to pay their passage. Many were crowded into the ship's hold in unsanitary conditions where cholera spread rapidly. Large numbers died on the voyage. Those who survived didn't have money to buy land. They found work as laborers; digging canals and building railroads. Between 1820 and 1870, half the population of Ireland emigrated to the U.S.

Another wave of political exiles came from the German states fleeing the crackdown that followed the pro-democracy uprisings of 1848.

The large numbers of these immigrants provoked considerable hostility. During the 1840s and 1850s, the American Party — better known today by their colloquial name of "Know Nothings" — ran candidates on an anti-immigrant platform. The Irish were accused of being terrorists and drunkards, the Germans of being Abolitionists (in the South) and Sabbath-breakers (in the North) and the Catholics in both groups were accused of plotting a Papist invasion which would destroy American liberty and impose an alien religious law. The party gained political power in some states, including Kentucky and Massachusetts. They also inspired vigilante violence, including an 1856 Election Day riot in Lexington, Ky., which left several German and Irish immigrants dead and many German and Irish homes and businesses looted and burned.

The Know Nothings lost power as political attention turned to the question of slavery. Both German and Irish Americans took a prominent part in the Civil War, and for a while after that, they were generally accepted as Americans. The Irish in particular, became citizens quickly and easily; like the Germans, they were white and therefore eligible for naturalization. Unlike the Germans, they all arrived speaking English. By the early 1900s, the Irish comprised the backbone of police forces and fire brigades. They also made up a formidable voting bloc. Soon after the Civil War, the reformer, newspaperman, and Union officer Carl Schurz became the first German-American senator.

In the 1880s, Italians and Russian Jews began to arrive in large numbers.

Both Columbus and the navigator Amerigo Vespucci, who gave his name to America, were Italian, and small numbers of Italian entrepreneurs and political refugees had been immigrating to the U.S. since the 1600s. Still, Italian-Americans made up a tiny fraction of the U.S. population until the 1880s brought a much larger number of Italians looking for work that paid a living wage, which was scarce at home. In the early years, 80% of Southern Italian immigrants were men, and 40-60% returned to Italy after earning and saving money in the U.S. [iii] Most of the nineteenth-century Italian immigrants, like the Irish, began as laborers — not merchants or landholders. Some took up factory work in the northern states. Many were active in labor movements, which their detractors took as evidence of their inherently violent and unruly nature, and their supporters as evidence of their passion for justice. Some Italian immigrants saved and start businesses of their own. Some moved South and became farmworkers; between 1860 and 1920, 64,000 Italians immigrated to Louisiana. Many of them prospered and became business owners, but this success was resented. In New Orleans in 1891, there was a mass lynching of Italians who had just been acquitted of killing a police officer. Many newspapers across the country blamed the victims and one open participant in the lynch mob later became governor of Louisiana. The federal government, however, condemned the killings and paid restitution to the families. (There was already an Italian-American, Francis Spinola, serving in Congress at this time.)

Russian Jews came fleeing from highly restrictive laws which confined them within "the Pale" and prevented them from owning land as well as from violent pogroms actively encouraged by the Russian government. Many of these immigrants were Socialists, used to organization, mutual support and a strong sense of government injustice. A large proportion of these immigrants settled in New York, worked in the textile industry or in sales and maintained tight-knit communities. They also worked hard at fitting into their new culture. Many families had refrained from learning Russian in the old country, confining themselves to Yiddish and Hebrew. But, they hastened to learn English in the U.S., sensing that it would increase their chance for acceptance and success in this new land. Many became involved in U.S. labor movements alongside the Italians. The children of these immigrants stayed in school longer and attended universities at a higher rate than in most other second-generation immigrant groups. This success was noted disapprovingly by some who objected either to their religion or their politics.

Immigration from Poland, Lithuania and other Eastern European countries also increased at this time. Native-born citizens who had become accustomed to Western European immigration began to express alarm again.

A lively debate raged in Congress and in newspapers across the land in the late 1880s. The Immigration Act of 1891 gave the federal government full authority over the admission or exclusion of immigrants and also over the naturalization of citizens. In 1892, the federal immigrant reception center opened at Ellis Island and replaced Castle Garden.

Between 1892 and 1920, the first major group of Middle Eastern immigrants passed through Ellis Island. Most of these immigrants came from what are now Syria, Lebanon and Palestine, where the decline of the silk industry was causing poverty and unemployment. The majority were Christians. Many came to the U.S. intending to earn money and return to their families in their native countries, but about two-thirds ended up staying in the U.S. and bringing their families to join them.

Throughout this period, U.S. employers continued to actively recruit European immigrants. Textile mills in the Northeast distributed fliers in German, Italian and other languages, urging workers to emigrate and better themselves. One popular illustration showed a workman wearing overalls and clutching a bag of gold. However, the reality immigrants encountered in the New World often failed to live up to the promises made to them.

The First World War brought renewed anti-immigrant hysteria, this time directed again at the Germans (and, to a much lesser degree, the Irish.) President Wilson passed laws against immigrants and dissidents strongly reminiscent of Adams' Alien and Sedition Acts. Many German immigrants were identified as aliens and deported, interned or surveilled. German-Americans were widely suspected of treasonous tendencies; some states passed laws banning the speaking of German in public, and the publication of German papers. Many German-Americans were beaten and humiliated by vigilant mobs and one Austrian was killed. Despite this, many German-Americans fought for the U.S. and after their return from the war, anti-German sentiment rapidly dissipated. But, thereafter, German-Americans were much less likely to conduct church services or publish papers in German; there was great emphasis on behaving like "real Americans."

12

After the war, a few anarchist bombings, many strikes and a great deal of talk about the need for social reform, sparked the first Red Scare. There was widespread fear, not only of anarchists, but also of Socialists of all stripes — Jews and Russians in particular — and non-English-speaking immigrants in general. This culminated in the Palmer Raids of January 1920, when thousands of Russian speakers, labor organizers and other suspected Communists were rounded up by policemen and volunteers from the American Legion and hundreds of immigrants were deported.

In 1924 a new immigration quota system was devised. The number of immigrants from any given nation in any given year could total no more than 2% of the number of foreign-born persons from that nation who lived in the U.S. in 1890 — before the major migration of Southern and Eastern Europeans.

As Hitler rose to power in Germany, there was a lively debate in the U.S. over whether Jewish refugees, especially children, should be accepted in numbers exceeding the quota set by the 1924 law. Some urged accepting them for humanitarian reasons; others described such an influx of immigrants as an invasion dangerous to the U.S. The nativists prevailed. One shipload of Jewish children was sent back from U.S. shores. Others never set out.

After the war, another lively debate broke out over immigration. The first changes dealt with people directly affected by the war. A 1945 law allowed war brides to rejoin their husbands in America; 1948 and 1953 laws provided for the immigration of refugees outside the quota system. Later, as the Cold War deepened, refugees from Communist countries were welcomed outside the quota system. The details of refugee resettlement have varied but refugee resettlement has been continuous.

There was also a broader debate. In the wake of Hitler's genocide, many Americans recoiled from the assumptions of racial superiority which had contributed to the national-origin immigration quota system. In the 1950s, there was a push by Northern politicians across party lines to end the quota system but this was defeated by more conservative Southerners of both parties. In the 1960s, as the domestic civil rights movement grew, there was a corresponding push for liberalized immigration policies. President Kennedy, himself the descendant of Irish immigrants, (once feared as dangerous and ethnically inferior), took up the cause of immigration reform. The reform bill was passed after his death in 1965.

The 1965 Immigration Act ended the quota system. The new system gave preference to family members of U.S. citizens, people with needed job skills, and refugees. This resulted in some increased immigration by Eastern European refugees fleeing Communist countries. But by the late 1900s, the face of immigration had changed. In the 1950s, more than half of all documented immigrants to the U.S. were European; in the 1990s that figure had fallen to 16%. In 1960, the U.S. population was 90% white. In 1990, that figure had fallen to 76%.

The 1965 reform brought another large wave of transatlantic migrants from the Middle East. Between 1967 and 2003, more than 750,000 immigrants arrived from the Arab world. Some were admitted as refugees; others as highly skilled workers wanted for crucial jobs. Many of the refugees also were highly skilled, though language and culture barriers, as well as trauma, made it hard for some to find employment in the fields in which they had excelled in their countries of origin.

Chapter Two

The Pacific Migration

Chinese immigrants began to arrive in significant numbers in the late 1840s. Some were fleeing the chaos and poverty spawned by the Opium Wars (in which Britain forced China to allow opium to be sold to her people.) Most of the early immigrants were men, coming alone to earn money and return to their families with enough money to secure property and live well. Some succeeded and came home prosperous and full of stories about the opportunities offered by America, the Land of the Golden Mountain. Others were inspired by their example to make the dangerous journey, leaving parents and spouses behind for years at a time — sometimes for a lifetime. Immigration increased through the 1850s and 1860s. Many Chinese immigrants worked in the mines and later, on the Union Pacific Railroad. The work was exhausting and dangerous; some of the railroad bosses said they couldn't find any other workers willing to take on what the Chinese would. Chinese railroad workers did organize successfully and won some improvements in their wages and living conditions.

Initially, these immigrants were generally welcomed. A California paper reported in 1852, "Quite a large number of the Celestials have arrived among us of late ... Scarcely a ship arrives that does not bring an increase to this worthy integer of our population ... [They] will yet vote at the same polls, study at the same schools, and bow at the same altar as our own countrymen."[iv] (It was not altogether clear how this was to happen, as a 1790 law reserved naturalization for "white" persons.)

But as the number of immigrants grew, so did the nativist backlash. Some white railroad workers objected to living and laboring alongside the Chinese. The bosses' retort that they could easily dispense with the white laborers and employ Chinese only, did not placate the white workers. Beginning in the 1850s, the California legislature taxed foreign miners. In 1875, the Page Law, ostensibly directed against the immigration of prostitutes, was widely used to prevent women from immigrating to join their husbands. In 1882, the federal government passed the Chinese Exclusion Act which forbade all immigration by Chinese workers of either gender. And in the 1880s, cities across the West Coast were swept by riots in which already-established Chinese residents were forcibly evicted, often beaten, sometimes killed and their homes and businesses either looted or destroyed. Local officials often turned a blind eye to the riots and sometimes took an active part in encouraging them. Some of the evictees resettled elsewhere on the West Coast and tried to sue for damages; others fled to Canada or back across the sea. The federal government, embarrassed and wanting trade deals with China, offered reparations to those evictees it could find.

As Chinese immigrants were turned away, other Asian populations were recruited to come to the U.S. Koreans began arriving after the signing of a U.S.-Korean treaty of amity in 1882. Small numbers of diplomats, merchants and students came at this time. In late 1800s, Japanese immigrants began to arrive. Many of them were younger sons whose older brothers were inheriting all the family land. Many brought their wives with them. This was encouraged by the Japanese government, which also tested emigrants to ensure that only literate and healthy people who would reflect well on their mother country left for the U.S. As Chinese laborers were excluded or expelled, West Coast employers sought Japanese workers, whom they initially praised as more obedient and tractable than the Chinese. As Japanese workers began to organize, Koreans were actively recruited as replacements.

Hawaii saw a particularly strong Japanese immigration. Between 1885 and 1924, 200,000 Japanese immigrants came to Hawaii, and nearly half of them stayed. In 1920, 40% of Hawaii's population was Japanese and Japanese schools, hot baths and Buddhist temples sprang up in many places. Seventy-five hundred Koreans also came to the island; first working in the sugar cane fields, then setting up as tenant farmers or shopkeepers.

In California, Asian immigrants made up a much smaller percentage of the population but still had a significant impact. Japanese farmers and farmworkers drained and improved large tracts of land, and by 1910, 70% of California's strawberries were grown by Japanese farmers or tenant farmers. Korean farm workers came to California in smaller numbers. In 1913, both groups suffered from vigilante violence and the passage of the Alien Land Act, which prohibited immigrants ineligible for citizenship — that is, nonwhites — from buying land. Koreans also were excluded from "whites-only" establishments, so many developed businesses serving their own people.

A 1908 treaty with Japan stopped the importation of contract laborers from Japan but allowed Japanese women to come join their husbands in the U.S. and promised that Japanese students would not be segregated in schools as Chinese students were. A 1905 Korean government decree temporarily stopped emigration to Hawaii.

In 1910, Japan occupied Korea, further complicating relationships between Korean and Japanese immigrants in the U.S. Ahn Chang-Ho, a prominent Korean-American leader, left the U.S. for Shanghai in 1932 to work in the provisional Korean government. Japanese forces captured him, and he died in prison.

From 1907 to 1917, many Sikhs immigrated from India to work, first in timber harvesting and railroad construction, then in agriculture. Only men arrived. Female immigrants were barred by the Page Act which had already limited the immigration of Chinese women. Many Sikh immigrants married Mexican women, creating a new cultural mix. In 1917, the Asiatic Barred Zone Act constricted even this limited immigration.

The 1924 Immigration Act which imposed strict quotas on European immigrants based on their national origin, took an even harsher approach to

Asian immigrants. The forthrightly titled "Oriental Exclusion Act," forbade the immigration of people legally ineligible for citizenship — that is, nonwhites.

During the Spanish-American War of 1898, the U.S. made common cause with freedom fighters in the Philippines trying to throw off Spanish colonial rule. Once the Spanish were gone, the U.S. set up its own military occupation and became the colonial power. President Taft encouraged educational connections between the two countries; many U.S.-born teachers traveled to the Philippines, and many Filipino students came to the U.S. In 1909, as Japanese farmworkers began to organize, Filipino farmworkers were recruited. Since Filipino immigrants came from several different ethnic groups and spoke different languages, it was harder for them to organize. In 1915, the government of the Philippines demanded legal protections for their emigrants in the U.S. Immigration slowed but picked up again in the 1920s. In 1935, the Philippines became a commonwealth rather than a colony, meaning that Filipino immigration was also barred under the Oriental Exclusion Act.

During the Second World War, Japanese-Americans were suspected of espionage; lack of evidence did nothing to calm these fears. More than 110,000 Japanese-Americans were taken from their communities, their businesses and their farms and settled in overcrowded internment camps. Some were relocated to Japan. Some were allowed to leave and settle further to the east. Most waited to be restored to the lives they had built. In 1944, the Supreme Court declared their internment to be unconstitutional but the last camp did not close until 1946. The U.S. government eventually paid well over a billion dollars in restitution.

The end of the war brought many political changes. Japan's occupation of Korea had ended and some Korean-Americans returned to Korea. One of these was Syngman Rhee, who immigrated from Korea, studied in the U.S.

and obtained his degree in international affairs from Princeton in 1910. He returned to Korea and became President, with U.S. backing, in 1948. The U.S. saw him as a staunch anti-Communist; many Koreans regarded him as a dictator and he was removed from power in a wave of protests in 1960. The Philippines also had been occupied by Japan during the war and at the war's end, the nation was declared independent. The Luce-Celler Bill of 1946 allowed the entry of 100 Filipino immigrants each year. Many more Filipino and Korean women immigrated as war brides, joining their U.S.-citizen husbands. Filipinos of both genders immigrated following a 1948 law allowing Filipino nurses to come to the U.S to study. Nearly 300,000 Korean children came to the U.S. for adoption. Some of them were war orphans; others were sent away by parents who could not afford to feed and clothe them in the lean time that followed the war.

The 1965 Immigration Act, which abolished the nationality-based quotas for European immigrants, also undid the Oriental Exclusion Act. Filipinos immigrated in high numbers since the new law favored medical workers and others with highly desired job skills. Koreans and Indian-Americans also immigrated in great numbers; some settling into high-level professional jobs, others into low-end white-collar work.

Chapter Three

Lines in the Sand: Crossing the Southern Border

Migration across the southern border begins with a story of illegal immigration followed by violent conquest and cultural eradication which might seem to be taken straight from the fears of ardent immigration opponents. But the immigrants in the case were Anglo-Americans.

In the early 1800s, Texas and California (which encompassed parts of what are now other Southwestern states) were Mexican territories. At first, Anglo-Americans could immigrate freely; Anglo immigrants to California were even awarded land grants if they took on Mexican citizenship and Catholicism. In 1830, Texas outlawed both slavery and Anglo immigration. But the law was not vigorously enforced and slave-holding Anglos continued to settle in large numbers. One of the ringleaders of the movement, Stephen Austin, declared that his "sole and only desire" was to "redeem [Texas] from the wilderness — to settle it with an intelligent honorable and interprising [sic] people," and urged his compatriots to forget about passports and come with rifles.ᵛ In 1836, the American settlers revolted and declared Texas a U.S. territory. In 1845, Texas was annexed to the U.S. and Texas and Mexico began to fight over exact location of the southern border of Texas. President Polk ordered federal troops onto the disputed land, blockaded the Rio Grande and described the subsequent Mexican attempt to dislodge them as an armed invasion and grounds for total war. The struggle that followed was ugly. Several U.S. officers wrote in dismay about the prevalence of murder, rape and robbery by the soldiers of their army.

In 1846, the fighting spread to California. In 1848, Mexico ceded the Southwestern territories to the U.S. Mexicans living on that land were allowed to remain and become U.S. citizens or to return to Mexico. Most remained, but with a great sense of loss. They complained of being disrespected by their Anglo neighbors, of having to speak English instead of Spanish to conduct necessary business and of feeling like "foreigners in their own land." A tax on "foreign" (meaning Mexican) miners was soon enacted in California, as was a supposedly anti-vagrancy act called "the Greaser Act," defining vagrants as persons "commonly known as Greasers or the issue of Spanish or Indian blood ... who went armed and were not peaceable and quiet persons." (Going armed was the norm for Anglos in that place and at that time.) In Texas, Mexican-American voting was discouraged by poll taxes and other measures.[vi] A Court of Private Land Claims established in 1891 overruled four-fifths of Mexican land claims. Many former landholders became laborers on Anglo farms. Some gave up and returned to Mexico.

In the early 1900s, Mexicans began to emigrate to the U.S. to work, despite ethnic hostilities. Unlike Asian or European immigrants, they were not restricted by ethnic quotas. Some Mexican-American immigrants were former landholders displaced by Mexican policies which allowed land grabs by large surveying companies. The poverty caused by these policies, along with quarrels over the civic role of the Catholic Church, led to civil war in Mexico and many more people crossed the Rio Grande to escape the violence. Between 1900 and 1930, the number of Mexicans in the southwestern U.S. jumped from 375,000 to more than 1,100,000. Like many Asian immigrants, they were welcomed as unskilled laborers but frozen out of higher-level positions. Many worked in construction or moved further north to do factory work. As Asian immigration was choked off, demand for Mexican farm laborers increased. Many were kept in debt by "company store" arrangements. Mexican-Americans tended to live in enclaves of their own, where they could be surrounded by their own language, enjoy their own food and avoid Anglo hostility at close quarters.

When the U.S. economy tanked in the Great Depression, President Herbert Hoover struggled to find a convincing explanation and solution. Part of his approach was to blame Mexicans for bringing down wages, putting U.S. laborers out of work and straining the resources of charities which should instead be focusing on the needs of U.S. citizens. This analysis did not lead to new legislation, but it did lead to an aggressive and indiscriminate program of deportation. Public employees with "Mexican-sounding names" were arrested and deported and obvious Anglos hired in their stead. Mexicans, Mexican-Americans and people with Latino surnames receiving any kind of public assistance were told that henceforth the only help they could get would be a ticket to take them south of the border. In Los Angeles, Calif., hospital patients who were, or appeared to be, of Mexican descent were removed from the hospital and taken out of the country, some of them on stretchers. There were also random raids on Latino parks and neighborhoods. The efforts were semi-official and haphazardly planned — and historians estimate that up to 60% of the people thus removed were U.S. citizens.[vii]

During the Second World War, as U.S. citizens were drafted to fight in great numbers and as the loss of European trade placed greater demands on U.S. food production, there was renewed demand for immigrant labor. The bracero program, signed into law in 1943, brought Mexican laborers in to work temporarily and then go back across the border. As President Truman's commission on migratory labor explained, "The demand for migratory labor is thus essentially twofold: To be ready to go to work when needed, to be gone when not needed."[viii] The Mexican government tried to stipulate wages and working conditions for braceros and at some points excluded Texas from the program because of widespread abuses by Texan employers. Many undocumented workers also came north, hoping for earnings like those of the braceros, and some braceros overstayed their official welcome. Many employers were glad to hire workers whose undocumented status effectively prevented them from protesting their pay or their working conditions.

After the war ended, many nativists resented the downward pressure on wages and the presence of "foreigners." They publicized individual crimes committed by undocumented immigrants and anti-Mexican sentiment spread rapidly. In 1954, President Eisenhower announced his grave concern over illegal immigration and responded to it with "Operation Wetback," a mass deportation program not too widely remembered until 2016 presidential candidate Donald Trump referred to it as a model for sane and humane immigration reform. During "Operation Wetback," The Border Patrol, the U.S. military and other law enforcement agencies made a concerted search for undocumented Mexicans, packed them onto buses, trains and ships and transported them back to Mexico. The government and the press exaggerated the size of the operation, hoping to scare more undocumented workers into fleeing south of their own accord. The actual deportees, regardless of the part of Mexico they called home, were taken far into the interior to prevent them from returning quickly to the U.S. Many were left in the Mexicali desert, where temperatures can rise to 125 degrees. On one hot July day, 88 people left there died of heatstroke.

In 1964, the year before coastal immigration was opened up again, concerns about exploitation of workers were raised and the bracero program was terminated. Many immigrants continued to come north without papers, either fleeing violence or seeking a way to support their families as political and economic chaos continued to devastate their home country. Employers embraced their labor; Anglo neighbors were more ambivalent.

Immigration from the rest of Latin America intensified during the political tumult of the 1960s-80s. The U.S. government was often willing to admit refugees from the Communist government in Cuba. Asylum seekers fleeing U.S.-backed anti-Communist governments found it much harder to gain legal status; given the urgent threat of death or "disappearance" at the hands of governments like Pinochet's. At the risk of being caught in the crossfire between government forces and equally ruthless leftist militias, many fled to Mexico and then into the U.S. without waiting to be legalized.

Part 2: American Responses

The previous section gave a brief chronological overview of American immigrants from different regions and of the changes in American immigration law. This section will take a deeper look at the American response to immigration.

There are many complex issues entangled in our narrative about immigration. Some are harder to discuss than others. People disagree about the impact of immigration on wages, workers' rights and the local economy, and on national security. These disagreements are based on differing readings of the facts and differing reasoning about strategies. But the discussion of immigration is also affected by attitudes which lie beyond reason. Our views on immigration draw deeply on our attitudes toward race and toward whomever and whatever we see as "Other." They are also profoundly influenced by our religious and moral principles. People on both sides of the debate tend to accuse the others of having no moral compass. In fact, there are strong convictions feeding all sides of the debate but they rest on different understandings of the world, of humanity, of God and of the nature of our moral obligations. The differences are so vast as to sometimes render people on different sides incomprehensible to one another. Finally, our views on immigration are shaped by our understanding of what America is and should be; we are as unlikely to be objective about this as about the nature of our families.

I attempt here to look at each of these factors in turn, at what has changed over the course of American history and what has remained constant. I begin, in Chapter Four, by acknowledging the elephant in the room — the issue of racial prejudice. Chapter Five considers immigration's economic impact, especially the relationship between immigrants and the labor movement. Chapter Six explores American perceptions of how immigration affects national security. The last two chapters return to the intangibles. Chapter Seven looks at how our religious principles or humanitarian ideals have shaped our view of immigration. Chapter Eight looks at the competing strands of American exceptionalism and at how our view of "American values" has shaped our understanding of who should become an American.

Chapter Four

Immigration and Race

Prominent clergyman A. Cleveland Coxe's essay "Government by Aliens" warns readers that "*To make a truly great nation ...* we are taught by history to demand (1) *a capable foundation of race*, (2) a fixed and *hereditary system of public morals,* and (3) a spirit of fidelity to national traditions and of adhesion to tried and long-established institutions ... The race-requisite has been supplied from our colonial era and has been, over and over again, put to severe tests ... *The race that gave birth to American nationality is the only race in history that has proved itself capable of self-government, or of creating and maintaining free institutions and laws that cooperate with freedom.*" (Emphasis mine.) He warns that the country is being overwhelmed by an unarmed yet still menacing invasion of immigrants who are both culturally and genetically incapable of free and peaceable self-governance. These aliens have committed atrocious acts of terror across the Atlantic and it may be surmised that they will soon begin to do the same thing in the U.S. They follow an alien religion — foreign to our shores and to our principles — and they seek to bend U.S. law to the dictates of that religion. "We give the invaders votes," he writes, "and they are soon drilled and magnified into a 'balance of power' which makes them our masters." Indeed, he says that they have already taken over one great U.S. city and imposed their alien religious law on it and they will soon do the same to the whole nation.[ix]

Coxe's essay was written in 1888. The "aliens" and "invaders" against whom he so strenuously warned his readers were Irish Catholics. It is curious to read Coxe's essay in 2017 when similar rhetoric is being deployed against largely Muslim immigrants from the Middle East and North Africa. Our definition of the racial Other, and our view of the sort of threat They pose has changed. The core idea that morals are hereditary, and that race determines and predicts character has been more durable.

There was a time, not long ago, when many Americans spoke confidently of entering a post-racial age. The language of white supremacy has never been entirely absent from our nation's airwaves or dinner tables but for a while it was possible for a certain segment of the American public (mostly the white progressive segment) to regard the speakers as embarrassing holdovers from the bad old days — increasingly irrelevant to our national life.

We now know better. In Barack Obama's second term, public outrage over police shootings of unarmed black people brought the question of race sharply and painfully to the nation's attention. The last election and the present administration have brought back overt appeals to the racialized fear of immigrants.

President Trump has described Middle Eastern immigrants and refugees as existential threats to national security and has repeatedly spoken of undocumented immigrants from across our southern border as rapists and drug dealers. His top adviser, Steve Bannon, is linked to a news organization which has published many articles on the superiority of Western culture and on the crimes committed by, and the supposed unfair advantages given to, people of color. Bannon has also expressed admiration for Jean Raspail's novel *The Camp of the Saints,* in which the white Christian West is taken over by hordes of nonwhite immigrants — described in viciously racist terms — who loot its treasures, destroy its institutions and sexually assault its women. The premise is one that might have made sense to Bishop Coxe, except that he would likely have seen Bannon, who comes from an Irish-

American Catholic family[3], as a member of the unwashed hordes rather than of the guardians of civilization.

Raspail's novel has also come up for praise by Congressman Steve King, who has also declared that "culture and demographics are our destiny ... we can't restore our civilization with somebody else's babies" and followed up on this statement by explaining that, "There are civilizations that produce very little freedom, if any. This western civilization is a superior civilization and we want to share it with everybody."[x] His remarks were promptly applauded by the Ku Klux Klan, a white supremacist organization with a long history of racial violence and an ongoing political presence.

Investigating the historical roots of American stories about race, particularly as they affect immigrants, is as urgent and relevant as it is likely to be painful.

Racial discrimination was built into American immigration law from the beginning. A 1790 law commanded that naturalization and citizenship should be limited to white persons. Since naturalization could be carried out by any municipal court, this initially allowed for varied interpretations of what it meant to be "white." African-Americans were clearly excluded. Irish-Americans, (however little Bishop Coxe, and some others liked them), were clearly included. The Chinese were widely held to be excluded but some courts were willing to naturalize them.

People judged as nonwhite could also be denied other rights, such as the right to testify in court. In 1854, California's Supreme Court heard a case in which a Chinese witness testified that some native-born Americans of European descent had murdered a Chinese man. The defense argued that the witness was not white and therefore could not testify. The Supreme Court upheld this argument and the men went free. Chinese-Americans, understandably appalled by this precedent, lobbied the federal government for protection.

---

[3] Obviously, Bannon's ethnic and religious background is not responsible for his views. The same background, after all, produced the Kennedy family, who championed the rights of immigrants and minorities.

Thanks in part to their influence, the 1870 Civil Rights Act guaranteed that "all persons" — of any race, citizens or noncitizens — should have "the same right" to "make and enforce contracts, to sue, be parties, give evidence, and to the full and equal benefit of all proceedings for the security of persons and property as is enjoyed by white citizens." [xi]

Citizenship, however, remained a thorny issue. The 14th Amendment to the Constitution, passed in 1868, promised citizenship to "all persons born or naturalized in the United States, and subject to the jurisdiction thereof." But the Attorney General later ruled that children born to "aliens" might not be fully "subject" to U.S. jurisdiction and therefore, not eligible for citizenship. The 1882 Chinese Exclusion act explicitly barred Chinese-Americans born in the U.S. from becoming citizens and after a 1923 Supreme Court ruling, previously naturalized Asian Indian-Americans were stripped of their citizenship. Mexicans in the territories seized by the U.S. were naturalized automatically and thus, were "white" in the eyes of the law. But, as detailed in Chapter Three, this did not necessarily secure them anything like equal protection.

In the early 1900s, the Dillingham Commission, charged by the government with researching immigrants to the U.S., came up with a *Dictionary of Races and Peoples*, explaining why some races were superior to others and therefore, should be privileged in admission to the U.S. They continued to discriminate among different European "races" which they saw as predisposed to certain character traits: Slavs were said to be prone to "fanaticism in religion, carelessness as to the business virtues of punctuality and often honesty;" Southern Italians to be "excitable, impulsive, highly imaginative, impracticable" and Scandinavians to be "the purest type." [xii] In 1917, following the Dillingham Commission's recommendations, a larger Asiatic Barred Zone was created, effectively stopping the immigration of most Asians. A literacy test was also imposed on European immigrants.

The 1921 and 1924 Immigration Acts went further, establishing national origin quota systems to ensure that the "pure types" predominated in the U.S. There was vigorous opposition to these laws, led by Emanuel Celler, a descendant of Jewish immigrants and a vigorous defender of racial equality.

"There is no such thing as superior and inferior races," Celler wrote in a letter to the editor. "One set of people is as good as another."[xiii] But most of his fellow statesmen disagreed. Indeed, some felt that the 1924 law did not go far enough. In 1927, prominent academics, including the President of Harvard, signed a petition to Congress to preserve the nation's genetic purity by including Mexico in the quota system. And, when some Americans pressed the U.S. to accept Jewish refugees fleeing Nazi persecution, opponents painted this attempt as a flagrant violation of the quota system and succeeded in blocking the admission of any Jewish refugees beyond the established quota.

As the U.S. moved toward involvement in the war against Hitler's powers, race prejudice began to seem like an embarrassment to the U.S. In 1941, President Roosevelt issued an edict declaring, "full participation in the national defense program by all citizens of the United States, regardless of race, creed, color, or national origin," based on "the firm belief that the democratic way of life within the nation can be defended successfully only with the help and support of all groups within its borders," and requiring that the federal government, unions and defense industries, "provide for the full and equitable participation of all workers." He set up a commission to hear complaints of ethnic prejudice in hiring and this group heard thousands of complaints each year. [4]

But after the war, the commission lapsed; complaints of discrimination increased, but the plaintiffs had no legal recourse. U.S. Senator Dennis Chavez expressed the outrage of some of his constituents: "If they go to war, they are called Americans — if they run for office, they are Spanish-Americans but if they are looking for jobs, they are referred to as damn

---

[4] The Second World War was not altogether a time of racial openness. As mentioned above, thousands of Japanese-Americans were interned. But this injustice was carried out in the name of national security, not racial superiority, as such. Chapter Six looks more closely at this.

Mexicans." He attempted to establish the Fair Employment Practices Commission on an ongoing basis but was voted down.[xiv]

In the decades following the war, the immigration quota system was relaxed and eventually ended. The black American struggle for civil rights also gave many immigrants from other ethnic groups greater equality before the law. When Emanuel Celler and allies tried to overturn the quota laws in 1951, they were voted down. The immigration bill passed at that time declared its intention of preserving "the social and cultural balance of the United States."[xv] But in 1965, President Kennedy and a group of reformers in the Senate, (including Celler), pressed for the abolition of the quota system, again using the language of civil rights. This time, after long struggle and negotiation, they prevailed. The 1965 law did away with national origin quotas. (Nativists did attempt backdoor ethnic entry control by placing a high priority on allowing entrance to immediate family members of people already in the U.S. But within a couple of decades, this "chain immigration" brought in many more non-Europeans than Europeans.) President Johnson, signing that law, declared that it "correct[ed] a cruel and enduring wrong in the conduct of the American nation." [xvi]

During the 1960s and 1970s, most immigration critics avoided using explicitly racial arguments, appealing instead to economic concerns about competition or environmental concerns about increased population. This respectable opposition didn't gain much popular traction. In the 1980s, some members of the anti-immigrant organization FAIR (Federation for American Immigration Reform) began to raise concerns about immigrants refusing to learn English or integrate into American culture. But the organization's executive director argued that, "If the only way to beat [immigration advocates] was to turn to animosity toward the racially and ethnically different immigrants, I wasn't willing to do that. I thought that was the one thing that would do more harm to America than the continuing immigration."[xvii]

But the appeal to ethnic fears generated much more enthusiasm than other concerns had. In 1995, British immigrant Peter Brimelow's book, *Alien Nation,* which played unabashedly to those ethnic fears, became a bestseller.

Brimelow argued that cultural and racial diversity led to fragmentation and civil war and that certain ethnic groups were intrinsically less able to reckon with consequences and control their impulses than others. Many other websites and books echoed Brimelow's sentiments, some in less respectable language. This rising wave of nativist sentiment augmented by the anti-terrorist alarms of the 2000s helped to fuel the explicitly nativist candidacy of our current president.

Throughout U.S. history, popular attitudes toward race have often lagged behind even the hesitant reforms and protections of the law. These attitudes manifested themselves in several ways — not always in opposition to immigration.

Some employers appealed to racial superiority to justify bringing in immigrants to do work "not fit for whites." A spokesman for the L.A. Chamber of Commerce explained in the early 1900s, that "the Mexican and Oriental" were obviously designed for stoop labor on farms because of "their crouching and bending habits," while naturally upright whites could not take the physical strain.[xviii] Another argued that "If society must have 'mudsills,' it is certainly better to take them from a race which would be benefited by even that position in a civilized community, than subject a portion of our own race to a position which they have outgrown."[xix] Many employers put these sentiments into practice by having native-born whites serve as foremen and overseers while employing members of the Lower Orders — first, Irish and Italian immigrants and later, Mexican or Asian immigrants —as common laborers.

Whites struggling to find and hold jobs, of course, did not always feel that they were being freed for better things. They often countered employer arguments with their own brand of racial propaganda. *The AFL Advocate*, in 1915, wrote about Mexican immigrants:

"Cheap labor, yes, at the sacrifice of manhood and homes and all that go to build up and sustain a community."

"Cheap labor — at the cost of every ideal cherished in the heart of the white race, utterly destroyed and buried beneath the greedy ambitions of a few grasping money gluttons, who would not hesitate to sink the balance of society to the lowest levels of animalism, if by so doing they can increase their own bank account." [The gluttons, presumably, were Anglo employers, and the animals, Latino workers ...]

"True Americans do not want or advocate the importation of any people who cannot be absorbed into full citizenship, who cannot essentially be raised to our highest social standard," they continued. [xx]

This seems to beg the question of what (besides the racial exclusion built into U.S. law) rendered people incapable of "our highest social standard," whatever that may be. What have native-born self-styled white Americans believed about immigrants?

For a while in the early 1900s, race prejudice was justified in terms of the so-called science of eugenics. Many U.S. academics, politicians and philanthropists embraced the ideas that humans should be selectively bred for improvement of the genetic stock and that Europeans were inherently more intelligent and responsible than others. At the 1923 opening of an international eugenics conference, the director of the American Museum of Natural History explained:

"In the U.S., we are slowly waking to the consciousness that education and environment do not fundamentally alter racial values. We are engaged in a serious struggle to maintain our historic republican institutions through barring the entrance of those unfit to share in the duties and responsibilities of our well-founded government. ... In the matter of racial virtues, my opinion is that from biological principles there is little promise in the melting-pot theory. Put three races together (Caucasian, Mongolian and the Negroid) you are likely to unite the vices of all three as the virtues. ... If the Negro fails in government, he may become a fine agriculturist or a fine mechanic. ... The right of the state to safeguard the character and integrity of the race or races on which its future depends is, to my mind, as incontestable as the right of the state to safeguard the health and morals of its peoples." [xxi]

Race-based immigration quotas were strongly supported by eugenicists along with sterilization of the unfit. Some states adopted laws allowing the forced sterilization of mental patients, prisoners, unwed mothers and others with undesirable genes. By 1936, over 60,000 people had been forcibly sterilized. Racial minorities and immigrants were especially likely to be targeted.

One great admirer of the U.S. eugenics program was Hitler, who wrote in *Mein Kampf*, "There is today one state in which at least weak beginnings toward a better conception [of citizenship] are noticeable. Of course, it is not our model German Republic, but the United States.[xxii]" When he came to power in Germany he passed eugenics laws closely based on U.S. models.

The Second World War and its aftermath turned the tide of popular opinion against U.S. eugenicists. Thereafter, racial hostility mostly abandoned the language of science and couched itself in terms of response to specific threats.

Sometimes immigrants have been accused of race-based squalor and lack of self-respect. In the late 1800s and early 1900s, many European immigrants who came without the money to buy land ended up in cities — which were expanding rapidly — sometimes at a pace beyond what their water and sewer systems could support. In 1891, a college president and economist declared the need to stop the flow of European immigrants, whom he described as "ignorant, unskilled, inert, accustomed to the beastliest conditions with little of social aspiration, with none of the expensive tastes for light and air and room, for decent dress and homely comforts."[xxiii] [5] A Congressman argued that Russian Jews and Italians, (then the most recent arrivals), "herd together like beasts and are disgraceful to civilization," and "should never have been allowed to come here."[xxiv] It is clear that poverty, hunger and disease plagued

---

[5] There is a long-standing tradition of distinguished Americans announcing that the poor simply do not want living space, health care or whatever else they lack. Possibly this removes a nagging sense of obligation which might otherwise trouble the prosperous.

the cities; it is less clear that this is due to the character traits, (race-based or otherwise), of the immigrants.

But educational and political advancement sometimes served to exacerbate, not to soothe, racial resentment. The rapid rise of second-generation Jews raised alarm in some quarters. In 1895, a self-styled white working man wrote to a newspaper to warn that, "The Russian Jews and the other Jews will completely control the finances and the government in 10 years, or they will all be dead ..."[xxv] In the 1920s, Henry Ford made similarly alarmist predictions about Jewish financiers and Jewish labor organizers. In the 1920s, Harvard President Abbott Lawrence Lowell attempted to restrict the admission of Jewish students to his college, remarking that, "the anti-Semitic feeling among students is increasing and it grows in direct proportion to increase in the number of Jews."[xxvi] In New England, Bishop Coxe was not the only person to express alarm at the fact that the Irish were successfully entering lawmaking and law enforcement in large numbers. In Hawaii, a vigorous debate about the education of second-generation Japanese-Americans sprang up, as sugarcane plantation owners complained that children were being taught too much for the station they were expected to occupy. When a mainland visitor to one plantation noticed Japanese children and asked the manager whether he thought they were capable of growing up into intelligent citizens, he replied, "Oh yes, they'll make intelligent citizens ... but not plantation laborers ... and that's what we want."[xxvii]

Sometimes immigrants have been described as racially predisposed to violence. The fear of immigrants' loyalty to their birth countries, or to "un-American'" political ideals, will be discussed in Chapter Six. Here we are simply considering the recurring idea that people from certain races or cultures are inherently more likely to commit murder.

This stereotype also was first applied to Europeans seen as "Other." In the 1880s, Coxe argued that the "Hibernian strain" was naturally lawless and violent. In the 1890s, newspapers justifying the lynching of Italians acquitted in a murder trial explained that Italians and Sicilians, who were accustomed to vendettas and mafia crimes, could not be peaceably absorbed into a law-abiding culture like that of the U.S. Therefore tighter immigration restrictions were called for.

Today's nativists also appeal to the fear of naturally violent races and cultures but they tend to appeal to a "Western civilization" which includes the Italians and Irish as representing the virtues of self-restraint and peaceful political change. More recently sweeping accusations of violence have been leveled against Latino and Middle Eastern immigrants. In 1954, an INS official supporting Operation Wetback explained, (without citing supporting evidence), that undocumented immigrants naturally considered themselves outlaws and went on to ever grosser violations of the law. President Trump used his first State of the Union speech to highlight violent crimes committed by undocumented immigrants.

It is undoubtedly true that some of these immigrants have committed armed robbery, assault and murder, and right-wing news sources tend to report these crimes extensively. It also appears that in our times, both documented and undocumented immigrants commit violent crimes less often than native-born citizens. Recent studies released by two different research groups with different political slants, found that immigrants were less likely to be convicted of or incarcerated for crimes than native-born citizens.[xxviii]Since undocumented immigrants are liable to arrest and conviction for purely immigration-related crimes such as re-entering the country without permission or driving without a valid license, it seems likely that their actual share of the violent crimes committed in the U.S. is even lower. But studies tend to be less effective than dramatic stories in driving popular opinion — and stories combined with preexisting prejudice have a very powerful effect.

Recently, U.S. political discourse has revived one of the ugliest and most visceral race-based accusations — the idea that men of other races are likely to rape white women. Fear of such assaults was often invoked to justify brutality against black American men from the days of slavery onward. It has also been invoked against immigrants.

In 1913, Leo Frank, born in the U.S. to Jewish parents, a factory owner and head of a Jewish fraternal order in Georgia, was convicted — after a long and fiercely contested trial — of raping and murdering a white girl in her early teens who worked at his factory. Some of the sensational newspaper coverage around the event emphasized Frank's Judaism. Frank was convicted, but not sentenced to death because there was still doubt as to whether the chief witness against him was actually the rapist and murderer. Frank was taken out of prison and lynched and in certain parts of the country, his death was described as justice. Half the 3,000 Jews in Georgia, (Frank's home state), fled after the lynching. The furor generated by the trial contributed to the formation of the Anti-Defamation League, but also to a revival of the Ku Klux Klan, which had long promoted the idea that white women were endangered by men of other races (among whom they included Jews.) Further evidence against Frank's accuser came to light later. Frank was pardoned posthumously and is widely considered to have been innocent.

Today, President Trump and certain portions of the nativist press promote a narrative about Mexican sexual predators; one typical article in Breitbart (formerly run by the President's former chief advisor Steve Bannon), lists several sensational cases of sexual assault by Mexican-Americans and explains that "deep and loving regard for women and our femininity is a purely Anglo-Saxon concept, inseparable from the very people who created our inherited culture — and implemented it wherever we settled and codified it into the civilizations we built," and explains that we must keep nonwhite people out in order to avoid becoming "a Third-World hellhole."[xxix] It is worth noting that earlier American white supremacists objected to Mexican men for precisely the opposite reason. During the U.S. invasion of Mexico — which ended in the seizure of the Southwestern territories — both U.S. officers and Mexicans lamented the high incidence of rape but the papers back home in the States told another story. Poems and articles portrayed Mexican women as longing for the embraces of Anglo-Saxon men because their own husbands were insufficiently energetic and virile, being overly fond of music, fruit and siestas. [xxx]

What are we to make of this constant fear whose catalysts shift so often? One theory is that racial fear is simply another manifestation of an inborn fear of the Other which may at some time have conferred a survival advantage. We fear them, not for anything particular that they are or do, but simply because they are not like us. The other theory is that in fact, we fear that they *are* like us — that we project the evil tendencies in our own hearts, or our own history onto other groups to avoid having to confront them in ourselves. This would make a certain kind of ugly sense of the changing narrative about Mexican-Americans.

Neither of these theories, of course, assume that the victims of such projections are wholly innocent. Certainly, immigrants have committed crimes in this country, just as native-born citizens have. By the same token, immigrants who suffer from racial prejudice have sometimes responded by joining the dominant culture's persecution of some racial group even further down in the pecking order. Often — but not always — this has taken the form of anti-black racism. One immigrant worker in the 1920s complained, "A group of us Mexicans who were well-dressed once went to a restaurant in Amarillo and they told us that if we wanted to eat we should go to the special department where it said, 'For Colored People.' I told my friend that I would rather die from starvation than to humiliate myself before the Americans by eating with the Negroes."[xxxi]

Throughout our history, there have also been Americans, (both immigrant and native-born), who were willing to work through their race prejudices and forge alliances across lines. In the early 1900s, Boston's Irish-American Mayor, James Curley, criticized Harvard for seeking to bar Jewish students, announcing, "God gave them their parents and their race, as he has given me mine. All of us under the Constitution are guaranteed equality, without regard to race, creed or color ... If the Jew is barred today, the Italian will be tomorrow, then the Spaniard and Pole and at some future date, the Irish." [xxxii] In 1952, as attempts at immigration reform were being struck down in Congress, Pulitzer Prize-winning historian (and child of Russian Jewish immigrants) Oscar Handlin wrote, "There ought to be no place in our laws for the racist ranking of nationalities ..." and looked back yearningly to a time when U.S. citizens "had confidence enough in their own society and in their own institutions to believe that any man could become an American. More than ever, do we now need to affirm that faith."[xxxiii]

Despite the statements of some current nativists, this inclusive attitude has never been held only by the elites. From the 1800s on, immigrant workers from different parts of the world came together in labor struggles which will be described in the next chapter.

Chapter Five

Immigration, Economics, and Labor

In the early days of the United States, most of the rational debate about immigration centered on economics. Immigration was handled by the Treasury Department and later by the Department of Labor and moved to the Department of Justice only in 1940.

How has immigration affected America's prosperity and America's native-born workers? The answers are complex, confusing and sometimes contradictory.

From the beginning, anti-immigration activists have been concerned about the possibility that immigrants might require financial help from native-born citizens. The earliest laws governing immigration from Europe excluded paupers, people suffering from physical or mental sickness or disability and all others deemed "likely to become a public charge." New immigrants who failed to find or keep work could be deported.

The U.S. is no longer in the habit of deporting legally admitted immigrants for being unemployed but federal welfare benefits are denied to all immigrants except green card holders and refugees who have been officially granted asylum. Even those immigrants must be in the U.S. for five years before they can apply for such benefits as Medicaid or food stamps. (Refugees do receive some initial assistance from federally funded resettlement agencies and some states make other assistance programs available to a broader range of immigrants.)

There is still much dispute about immigrants receiving government benefits. As usual, both sides can show some statistics to back up their cases. The Center for Immigration Studies (CIS), which lobbies for reduced immigration, recently published a study showing that 51% of households headed by immigrants (documented or undocumented) received some form of government assistance in 2012, while a smaller percentage of non-immigrant-headed households received assistance. They have used this study as the basis for appeals to reduce immigration because it places an undue burden on native-born taxpayers.[xxxiv]

Other groups have challenged CIS's way of grouping and reporting the data. Since the CIS study described any household in which any member receives any form of assistance as being "on welfare," most of the assistance they measured goes to American-born children of immigrants — that is, to U.S. citizens. And households listed as "receiving welfare" may get only very limited benefits, such as reduced-price school lunches for children or subsidized health care for an American spouse.

A 2010 study by the pro-immigration group the American Immigration Council found that immigrants "earn about $240 billion a year, pay about $90 billion a year in taxes and use about $5 billion in public benefits." They suggested that in fact, immigrants are funding social safety nets for citizens.[xxxv]

There is much more agreement on the other major economic impact of immigrants. For the past three centuries, immigrant labor has been a major driver of the U.S. economy. In the mid-1800s, the great transcontinental railroad was built largely with immigrant labor — Irish immigrants working from the East and Chinese immigrants from the West. In the early 1900s,

European immigrants in the East powered the textile mills and steel factories that brought the Industrial Revolution fully into the New World and Asian and Latino immigrants in the South and West cleared forests, drained swamps and established productive agricultural land. Today, immigrants still do vital jobs which native-born citizens are less willing to take on. U.S. agriculture continues to rely heavily on the labor of Latino immigrants, documented and undocumented. U.S. medicine also relies heavily on immigrants. A recent study found that one-quarter of U.S. physicians are foreign-born and that these physicians are concentrated in rural and low-income areas which tend to be underserved.[xxxvi]

First-generation immigrants also tend to be people with high levels of initiative and willingness to start new things; as they settle into the U.S., this often manifests as an entrepreneurial spirit. A 2009 study found that immigrants were slightly more likely to be self-employed than native-born citizens, much more likely if factors such as wealth and education levels are factored in.[xxxvii] A survey of engineering and tech startups between 2006 and 2012 found that 25% of startups had at least one founder who was foreign-born.[xxxviii]

Opponents of immigration tend to concede the great productivity of the immigrant workforce. But many argue that this productivity comes at the expense of U.S. workers who might be able to demand better working conditions and higher pay if there were no competition from immigrant workers with less stringent demands. This argument has a strong historical basis.

Throughout U.S. history, employers have taken advantage of the cheap labor offered by the newest and poorest immigrants. The textile mills of New England chiefly employed native-born citizens in the mid-1800s. By the early 1900s, most employees were Irish and German immigrants. When these went on strike seeking better wages or slower machine speeds that allowed for safer work, many strikers were dismissed and replaced with Italian and Polish workers.

Ethnic tension was also encouraged by the widespread practice of overt racial segregation of jobs. In 1904, the Hawaiian Sugar Planters' Association resolved that all skilled or supervisory positions should be held by people eligible for citizenship — that is, by people considered "white." Similar arrangements existed in the Southern states to keep black and Latino workers out of highly-skilled and highly-paid positions

Immigrants of other races were more often described as racially suited for doing low-wage work. In the late 1800s, mine owner Sylvester Mowry wrote that "the lower class of Mexicans ... are docile, faithful, good servants ...They have been 'peons' for generations. They will always remain so, as it is their natural condition."[xxxix] Mowry and many other mine owners paid Mexican workers about half what they paid white workers for identical jobs. Japanese workers were similarly praised as more docile and less demanding than Chinese workers in the first years of Japanese immigration. When Mexican and Japanese immigrants began to organize and make demands, employers began to look for new immigrant groups to replace them. Some decided that their best leverage was in diversity: "Keep a variety of laborers — that is different nationalities — and thus prevent any concerted action in case of strikes, for there are few, if any, cases of Japs, Chinese and Portuguese entering into a strike as a unit," one Hawaiian plantation manager wrote in 1896[xl]. In the early 1900s, Koreans were brought in to replace a large portion of the organized Japanese workers. When the Korean government restricted immigration, Filipinos were brought instead.

Despite all this, immigrants began to organize across racial and cultural barriers. In 1903, 200 Mexican workers in California joined a much larger number of Japanese workers in a strike to demand higher piecework rates. This spontaneous collaboration led to the formation of the Japanese-Mexican Labor Association. They succeeded in getting their demands met.

In 1909, Japanese workers went on strike and demanded to be given the same wages as Portuguese workers. Strike leaders were jailed, and no official concessions were made ... but soon after work resumed, some wage raises were granted. The planters, growing wary of the organizing tendencies of their

Japanese employees, brought in more Filipino workers. The Filipinos formed a worker's association of their own but for a while, planters were able to play the two groups off against each other. Then in 1919, both groups voiced their grievances at once. The Japanese association sent a letter which read in part, "We hear that there are in Hawaii, over a hundred millionaires; men chiefly connected with the sugar plantations. It is not our purpose to complain and envy, but we would like to state that there are on the sugar plantations which produced these large fortunes for their owners, a large number of laborers who are suffering under a wage of 77 cents a day."[xli]

They requested a wage increase, an eight-hour instead of 10-hour workday, maternity leave and overtime pay. All demands were rejected. The Japanese workers repeatedly requested meetings with the plantation owners. The Filipino workers went on strike in January and four days later the Japanese workers joined them.

The English press ran articles about the threat posed by "alien agitators;" one editorial asserted that, "An American citizen who advocates anything less than resistance to the bitter end against the arrogant ambition of the Japanese agitators is a traitor to his own people." The planter's association certainly resisted firmly. Strikers were evicted from their homes in February, in the middle of a flu epidemic. Many evictees died. The English press said that the sufferings of the Filipinos resulted from their letting the Japanese use and deceive them. The head of the Filipino association called off the strike, but many Filipinos stayed out anyway, and soon their leader agreed to declare the strike officially on again. The planters hired native Hawaiian, Korean and Portuguese workers to take the place of strikers, and the strike ended in apparent failure in July, when the strikers either returned to work or left the island. Labor leaders were blacklisted and could not have found work if they wanted it. Still, shortly after the strike, wages were raised and housing improved.[xlii]

These Hawaiian strikes arose spontaneously and were not tied to any long-established labor organization. But during the late 1800s and early 1900s, various organized labor unions formed and pressured employers for better pay and working conditions. Different unions handled the question of immigration and race in very different ways.

The first major organization was the Knights of Labor, which began as a secret society on the East Coast in 1869, but soon went public and spread across the country. The Knights welcomed workers of all wage and skill levels. Black Americans were part of the Knights organization, although they met in segregated chapters. The Knights demanded equal pay for equal work as well as eight-hour days, the outlawing of child labor and a graduated income tax. Their idea was to unite long-established populations of American workers in pressing for systemic reform. New immigrants were treated as threats and competitors, not potential members. The Knights opposed Asian immigration and supported the Chinese Exclusion Act as well as the Contract Labor Act.

The Knights' leader, Terence Powderly, supported boycotts and negotiations with company managers but he opposed strikes. His members didn't necessarily follow his lead. Many joined a strike for the eight-hour day in Chicago in May 1886. Strikers were locked out and tumultuous protests began; the police used considerable force to disperse strikers. The following evening, an anarchist group headed by a native-born former Confederate soldier turned civil rights worker and a highly educated German immigrant with strong working-class sympathies, called a meeting in Haymarket Square to protest what they termed "police brutality." Police described the meeting as fairly quiet but nevertheless, illegal. They ordered the crowd to disperse. Somebody threw a bomb, the police began shooting, and in the end, seven policemen and two strikers were dead and many more injured.

The press carried articles about violent foreign agitation. Two hundred protestors were arrested. Four of them, (three being German immigrants), were hanged, not because they were shown to have built or thrown the bomb (no one ever traced that) but because their message was believed to have incited violence. The legislature banned eight-hour workdays. The Knights of Labor, which included many European immigrants, came under considerable suspicion as a hotbed of alien anarchist agitation. Its numbers and influence declined rapidly.

The first major group to step into the vacuum was the American Federation of Labor (AFL), established in 1886. Like the Knights, the AFL sought wage improvements, an eight-hour workday and an end to child labor. Also, like the Knights, they had a vision of economic justice for all. The preamble to their Constitution states, "A struggle is going on in all the nations of the civilized world between the oppressors and the oppressed of all countries, a struggle between the capitalist and the laborer, which ... will work disastrous results to the toiling millions if they are not combined for mutual protection and benefit ..."[xliii] "But Samuel Gompers, their leader, made it very clear that this was an all-American, law-abiding, patriotic group which had no truck with anarchists or agitators. As he later explained to Congress, "it is our duty to live our lives as workers in the society in which we live and not to work for the downfall or the destruction or the overthrow of that society."[xliv] In practical terms, this accommodation to the existing society appeared in the form of race and class limitations.

Only higher-skilled and higher-paid workers were admitted to the AFL's craft unions. Given the widespread practice of barring nonwhite workers from higher-level employment, this meant that the AFL was essentially an all-white union. (The notable exception was the United Mine Workers, which was affiliated with the AFL but included lower-paid workers, many of them black.)

Gompers' opposition to immigration increased with time. In 1883, he wrote that, "I have no objection to the people of any country coming to America, Chinese excepted (I am not so sentimental as all that ...)" By the early 1900s, he had broadened his objections: "Our fellow workmen living on the Pacific Coast and Hawaii realized the danger that not only threatened but confronted them from Chinese, Korean and other Mongolian laborers, and the American Federation of Labor conventions declared that efforts should be made to extend the exclusion laws or to bring about some exclusion of Oriental laborers coming to the United States and its possessions ..." By 1923, his concern extended to many Europeans: "The greater the number of immigrants, the less American the United States becomes ...The American Federation of Labor believes that the foreigners now in this country should be assimilated before others are permitted to come except such countries as Great Britain, France, Germany and Scandinavia. Those who would flood the country with hordes of immigrants from southeastern Europe care no more for America than do the Hottentots. Their desires are governed by greed."[xlv]

The Japanese-Mexican Laborers Association (JMLA)applied for AFL membership just after its successful 1903 strike. Gompers agreed to take them on as charter members — on one condition: "Your union will under no circumstances accept membership of any Chinese or Japanese." J.M. Lizarras, leader of the Mexican workers in the association, replied, "In the past we have counseled, fought and lived on very short rations with our Japanese brothers, and toiled with them in the fields and they have been uniformly kind and considerate. We would be false to them if we now accepted privileges for ourselves which are not accorded to them ... We will refuse any other kind of charter, except one which will wipe out race prejudice and recognize our fellow workers as being as good as ourselves." No charter was granted. [xlvi]

The JMLA dispersed in a few years. The AFL continued to grow and to work within the system. Gompers brought the AFL into cooperation with the National Civic Federation, a group largely made up of business owners who were willing to allow collective bargaining and make workplace reforms in the interest of preserving peace and the established system

But Lizarras was not the only labor organizer who valued inter-ethnic solidarity. In 1905, the Industrial Workers of the World laid out a vision of labor organizing significantly different from the AFL's. The preamble to their constitution declared, "We find that the centering of the management of industries into fewer and fewer hands makes the trade unions unable to cope with the ever-growing power of the employing class. The trade unions foster a state of affairs which allows one set of workers to be pitted against another set of workers in the same industry, thereby helping defeat one another in wage wars ... " And they laid out a revolutionary, rather than reformist, agenda for change: "There can be no peace so long as hunger and want are found among millions of the working people and the few, who make up the employing class, have all the good things of life. Between these two classes, a struggle must go on until the workers of the world organize, take possession of the earth and the machines of production, and abolish the wage system ... Instead of the conservative motto, "A fair day's wage for a fair day's work," we must inscribe on our banner the revolutionary watchword, "Abolition of the wage system.""[xlvii][6]

From the beginning, the IWW reached out to Asian-American immigrants and included black and white workers in the same chapters. The Japanese activist Shinziro Kotoku spent time with the Wobblies (as IWW members were colloquially called) in 1906 and returned to Japan inspired by the idea of general strikes and mass direct action. Authorities in the U.S. and Japan kept a wary eye on groups so openly revolutionary in their aims.

The conflicts between the AFL and the IWW, in their economic vision and view of immigrants, became sharply visible in the dramatic textile strikes of 1912. The best known of the strikes was the so-called Bread and Roses Strike in Lawrence, Mass. The mills in Lawrence, and indeed throughout the Northeast, employed large numbers of immigrants. The longer-established Irish and Germans tended to have the most skilled and best-paid jobs. Some of these belonged to AFL-associated craft unions. The low-wage work was largely done by Italians, Poles, Russians, Syrians and other recent arrivals who had no access to the AFL unions. The work was dangerous; people routinely lost limbs to the spinning and weaving machines or were crushed by the cranes in the unloading rooms. The pay was low enough so that many workers were tightly packed into overcrowded and unsanitary tenements. The average life expectancy for a mill owner in 1912 was 58; for a millhand, 36.

The Wobblies began by persuading low-wage workers at each mill to establish a common fund to pay the living expenses of sick workers, so they

------

[6] This is the 1908 update to the Preamble, which fleshes out what was only sketched in in the 1905 version.

were more able to stay home, rather than trying to work and running a higher risk of major injury. People from all nationalities contributed to and benefited from, the fund. With this much solidarity established, it was easier to envision bolder forms of concerted action. A long-anticipated pay cut in January 1912 sparked a strike. Workers shouted "Short pay! All out!" and marched out of the factories, sometimes breaking the machinery as they went — sometimes, also, grabbing people who meant to keep working and dragging them outside, too. The strike began in one mill but soon spread across the city.

The propaganda battle began almost as soon as the strike. City leaders deplored rioting and called in militia companies. Conservative newspapers blamed foreigners: "The textile operatives in many of the mills number a larger percentage of foreigners — Italians, Syrians, Portuguese, Poles and Armenians — than of any English-speaking race ... these classes of men and women now overrun the place ... ignorant and easily deceived and more readily excited."[xlviii] IWW leader Joseph Ettor, brought in haste to organize the unfolding strike, appealed to inter-ethnic unity: ""Forget that you are Hebrews, forget that you are Poles, Germans or Russians. Among workers, there is only one nationality, one race, one creed." He added to the skilled workers, "You are the skilled of the mills. Do not play the aristocrat because you speak English, are habituated to the country, have a trade and are better paid. Throw in your lot with the low-paid. You must either reach down and lift them up or they will reach up and pull you down."

John Golden, president of the AFL's United Textile Workers, tried to keep his skilled workers out of the strike. Many ignored his advice and walked out. Samuel Gompers called the strike, "class conscious industrial revolution ... a passing event that is not intended to be an organization for the protection of the immediate rights or promotion of the near future interests of the workers," but he defended the rights of the I.W.W. members to, "express themselves as their conscience dictates."[xlix] But as the strike went on for weeks, then months, it became harder to keep a neutral stance.

Ettor and his fellow organizer, Italian-born Arturo Giovanitti, preached nonviolence but this wasn't always carried out in practice; many were injured in scuffles between strikers and strikebreakers (often both Southern

European immigrants, desperate to make ends meet and differing about how best to do that) or strikers and police (largely Irish) or strikers and militia members (many of them volunteers from Harvard.) There were two deaths — a boy taking part in a strikers' parade who was chased across icy sidewalks by militia and accidentally stabbed with a bayonet, and a woman bystander at an altercation who was shot, no one knew by whom. When the police followed a tip, and found a large cache of dynamite, commentators warned about violent foreign anarchists and many immigrants were arrested on suspicion. Those immigrants were quietly released when new evidence suggested that the dynamite had actually been purchased and planted by the man who had told the police where to find it. That man, the son-in-law of the man who owned most of Lawrence's mills, committed suicide before going to trial. Martial law was declared. Strikers began to send their children out of the city to pro-labor people who could better afford to feed them. The militia forbade this exodus, and there was an ugly skirmish at the train station in which some women and children were beaten by police trying to prevent their departure. The press became frantic, and Congress decided to hold hearings on what had made the workers so desperate.

The hearings began with testimony from workingmen at the mills, describing wages that left them living on bread and molasses in cold crowded rooms, also describing excessive use of force by the police. A Lawrence official testified that the strikers were understating their wages and Golden of the AFL testified that the IWW taught violence and poisoned the minds of the poor. Several shouting matches ensued. Finally, the strike committee brought on another set of witnesses: children, some as young as thirteen, who worked in the mills. They described wages and conditions and injuries from the machines; when asked about studies, about play ... they looked blankly at their interlocutors. [7]

---

[7] One example of the children's testimony is online at http://historymatters.gmu.edu/d/61/

Public sympathy swung sharply to the strikers. The mills abruptly granted the demands of strikers and work resumed. It was a victory for the workers and the Wobblies. But the battle for the narrative was not over. The Lawrence Citizens' Association published a pamphlet entitled, *Reign of Terror in an American City,* which described the IWW as a terrorist organization which sent "swarthy men" to terrorize hardworking families into staying out of work. The IWW, meanwhile, had moved on to other strikes.[1] Some of these were more violent and less successful than Bread and Roses had been. A few ended in gun battles in which each side claimed to have been exercising justifiable self-defense against aggressors.

During the First World War, the AFL's power grew while the IWW's waned. The government, eager to speed wartime production, supported the AFL's style of collective bargaining in order to keep workers on the job. President Wilson appointed Gompers to a council designed to encourage labor support for the war effort. The IWW tended to portray the war as a pointless imperialist struggle and urged workers to stay out of it. Many IWW leaders were arrested and given lengthy prison sentences under the newly revived Sedition Act. The IWW's internationalism was also seen as suspect. Chapter Six will examine the revival of nativism brought about by the war.

After the war, the IWW and the position of immigrant workers were further weakened by the first Red Scare. After anarchist leaflets and bombs were mailed to prominent politicians, the government cracked down on suspected anarchists, Communists and immigrants. (This will be described at greater length in the next chapter.) This political pressure, combined with internal divisions over how to respond to state-sponsored communism in Russia, considerably weakened the IWW. The group never died out and never lost its cosmopolitan vision, but they did lose numbers and today, when the position of labor is discussed, people are usually thinking of the AFL-CIO.

In 1924, the AFL went through a crisis of its own. With Samuel Gompers dead, a new leader was needed; one without a strong IWW influence to push back against. Some AFL leaders began to feel the need to reach out more fully to immigrants, black Americans, and low-wage workers, while others felt that this would push them dangerously close to radicalism. In 1935, the Committee for Industrial Organization (CIO) began to set up industry-wide and ethnically inclusive unions for farm workers, factory workers and others who had never been admitted into the AFL. A 1941 auto strike attracted large numbers of black workers to the union. The CIO began as an AFL branch but was ejected from the AFL in 1937. The organizations worked together to re-elect Franklin Delano Roosevelt and lobby for worker protection. The CIO, like the IWW, made extensive use of strikes and pushed hard for civil rights. However, their leadership tended to be anti-Communist and they were more apt to speak of fair wages than of overturning the wage system.

After the Second World War, as the full horrors of Hitler's ethnic cleansing programs were revealed and ethnic prejudice lost its respectability, labor took an active role in desegregation. In 1955, the AFL and CIO merged, and the new AFL-CIO welcomed members of all races.

In the 1960s, the United Farm Workers movement brought largely Hispanic farm workers together to demand better working conditions and to call for the end of the bracero program which brought Mexican laborers into the U.S. on a temporary contract basis. This opposition was based, not on anti-Mexican sentiment, but on a concern for the harsh conditions in which braceros worked. Cesar Chavez, the UFW's leader, was the son of migrant workers himself and described their working conditions as akin to slavery. After the program was ended, Chavez continued to organize boycotts and strikes to win better conditions for farmworkers — whether naturalized citizens or migrants. The UFW was welcomed into the AFL-CIO.

The AFL-CIO, in a sharp reversal of the AFL's early policies, supported the 1965 immigration act which dismantled the ethnic quota system altogether. In 1990, the AFL-CIO advocated a legal path to citizenship for undocumented immigrants. The organization's commitment to supporting workers' rights within the present economic and legal system has not changed. Nor, perhaps, has the concern voiced in the AFL's 1915 letter quoted in the previous chapter, which stated that no good could come to the worker from the importation of laborers who could not become citizens. But the proposed remedy has changed. Instead of excluding immigrants from different ethnic backgrounds, the largest representative of American labor has decided instead to advocate for welcoming immigrants and conferring on them the rights and privileges of citizenship.

Chapter Six

Immigration and National Security

One of the most persistent arguments against immigration is that immigrants undermine the United States' political stability and national security. This argument has taken different forms in different times.

U.S. involvement in foreign wars has repeatedly raised concerns about whether immigrants from hostile countries are loyal to the U.S., or to the lands where they were born. U.S. history includes some immigrants who reverted to their original loyalties during wartime and many others who were punished for false assumptions about their loyalties.

In the early 1900s, German immigrants, who had been arriving in large numbers for over a century, were accepted by many Americans who were still leery of newer waves of immigration from southern Europe. Their heavy involvement on the Union side of the Civil War, the long Senate career of Union veteran and perpetual reformer Carl Schurz, and a general reputation for hard work and orderliness were all in the Germans' favor. There were also some lingering concerns over their clearly separate ethnic identity.

There were more than 800 German-language newspapers in the U.S. Many Germans attended German-language churches; many German men spent time at all-German social clubs. Americans who saw the U.S. as an Anglo-Saxon nation worried that this showed an un-American refusal to assimilate.

The First World War brought those tensions to a head. Understandable outrage over reports of atrocities committed by occupying German forces in Belgium bled over easily into furious declarations that their race was to blame. After the shooting of English nurse and aide to fugitives Edith Cavell, the U.S. minister to Belgium declared, "For one of our Anglo-Saxon race and legal traditions to understand conditions in Germany during the Belgian occupation, it is necessary to banish resolutely from the mind every conception of right that we have inherited from our ancestors ... In the German mentality these conceptions do not exist; the Germans think in other sequences, they act according to another principle, if it is a principle ... the conviction that there is only one right, one privilege, and it belongs exclusively to Germany; the right, namely, to do whatever they have the physical force to do ..."[8]

As the U.S. mobilized for war, the government moved to control public opinion. The Sedition Act of 1918 made it unlawful to "insult or abuse" the U.S. government or the war, to interfere with wartime production, or to speak in a way that encouraged such actions. Many socialists and pacifists received ten-year sentences for seditious speech. At the same time, the government's so-called "Committee for Public Information" worked with artists as well as businesses to promote a pro-war and anti-German narrative. Films like *The Kaiser: The Beast of Berlin,* and *To Hell with the Kaiser,* sold out rapidly. The CPI's posters and pamphlets depicted both real and imagined German atrocities — the crucifixion of a captured Canadian

---

[8] The minister's outrage is easy to understand. But the same vicious principle seems to appear in the actions of the American Anglo-Saxons who violently dispossessed the Native Americans, and then the Mexicans in California and Texas.

airman was a particularly gut-wrenching example of the latter. One historian writes that, "After the war, Edward Bernays, who directed CPI propaganda efforts in Latin America, openly admitted that his colleagues used alleged atrocities to provoke a public outcry against Germany. Some of the atrocity stories which were circulated during the war, such as the one about a tub full of eyeballs or the story of the seven-year-old boy who confronted German soldiers with a wooden gun, were actually recycled from previous conflicts."[lii]

The CPI and other agencies also encouraged patriotic Americans to keep an eye out for domestic traitors and saboteurs. This fear was not completely unfounded. Before the U.S. entered the war, several of its ships carrying munitions to Britain were sunk by mysterious explosions. It eventually became clear that some of the ships had been deliberately sunk by bombs packed into the cargo by saboteurs. And in 1916, German agents set fires at the Black Tom munitions plant in New York Harbor, causing a spectacular explosion that shook the ground with earthquake force, killed several people (different reports give different numbers, none over ten), and destroyed a great deal of war materiel. Responsibility for the blast was not satisfactorily settled until long after the war was over. In the meantime, there was a great deal of unfocused fear, suspicion and hostility.

Some of this hostility was directed against German-Americans who were publicly and nonviolently opposed to the war. Many of the early German immigrants who came to the U.S. seeking religious freedom were pacifists; many of the political idealists who left Germany after the suppression of the 1848 uprising were skeptical of what they saw as a needless imperial war. Some members of both groups urged young men not to join the Army and urged munitions workers to strike. This was sedition under the new laws and was punished as such. Some newspaper writers speculated that pacifism was actually a front for a more sinister pro-German plot.

Many German-Americans who did not oppose U.S. participation in the war still fell under suspicion simply because of their ethnicity. The government took some official steps against German-Americans; interning or deporting German nationals or German-born nationals of other countries. German-born Boston Symphony Orchestra conductor Karl Muck was interned for a year, although he was a Swiss citizen. The same thing happened to the Austrian-born conductor of the Cincinnati Symphony, although there was no evidence that either man was engaged in pro-German activities. Ohio, Nebraska and Iowa forbade the teaching of German. Many schools and libraries in other states dropped German classes and pulled German books from the shelves. The government confiscated the property of hundreds of German citizens residing in the U.S. — and after the war, sold that property to U.S. citizens, which was called "Americanizing it."[liii]

Some citizens went further in taking matters into their own hands. In many cities, Germans were bullied into buying war bonds — some enthusiasts went so far as to beat those who refused or strip them and wrap them in the American flag. And in April 1918, Austrian-born socialist Frank Prager was stripped, beaten, flag-wrapped and hanged by a mob. Some newspapers condemned this vigilantism. Others described it as a sign of patriotic spirit.

Despite all this, German-Americans volunteered to fight in the U.S. Army. They were watched over vigilantly but some achieved great distinction on the battlefield — and many died fighting for the country that mistrusted them.

As the Second World War loomed and Jews fled Germany and Austria ahead of Hitler, national security concerns were invoked to prevent their entry into the U.S. in large numbers. German and Austrian Jews, opponents argued, were nevertheless Germans and Austrians and their numbers might include spies or saboteurs eager to strike against the U.S. President Franklin Delano Roosevelt slightly raised the German and Austrian quotas but he took no other action. Many Jews were interned and killed because they found no country to take them in. There are uncomfortable parallels to the U.S.'s current reluctance to accept Middle Eastern refugees.

For a long time, the U.S. hesitated on the edge of war. Japan's surprise attack on Pearl Harbor catapulted the nation into war — and prompted vengeance against Japanese-Americans who bore no responsibility for the attack.

Japanese-Americans had always occupied a more marginal place than German-Americans in U.S. society. Japanese immigrants were not allowed to become U.S. citizens, though their U.S.-born children had birthright citizenship. In the furor that followed the bombing of Pearl Harbor, the general in charge of defending the West Coast, John DeWitt, argued, "A Jap's a Jap. They are a dangerous element, whether loyal or not." [liv] J. Edgar Hoover and other federal officials charged with security thought this warning overblown but they did not stop DeWitt. Armed with this sketchy justification, the government began to round up Japanese-Americans on the West Coast within 48 hours of the Pearl Harbor attack. In many cases, the press supported the roundups. *The L.A. Times* wrote, "A viper is nonetheless a viper wherever the egg is hatched — so a Japanese-American, born of Japanese parents — grows up to be a Japanese, not an American." [lv] In the end, 110,000 men, women and children were taken from their homes and businesses and locked in squalid, overcrowded internment camps. U.S. citizenship offered no protection. The camps were surrounded by barbed wire and patrolled by armed guards.

Hawaii's population included 150,000 Japanese–Americans, and Hawaii's governor refused to intern them. For one thing, such a move would have crippled Hawaii's economy and its contribution to the war effort. Honolulu's Chamber of Commerce pointed this out and Hawaiians seemed more willing to recognize the Japanese as their fellow Americans. The head of the Chamber observed that "The citizens of Japanese blood would fight as loyally for America as any other citizen ..." and the superintendent of public education for the state told teachers, "The most helpless victims, emotionally and psychologically, of the present situation in Hawaii, will be children of Japanese ancestry and their parents ..." [lvi]

But on the mainland, there was no such solidarity. It was only in December 1944, after fierce court battles, that the interment orders were rescinded. By then, many of the released Japanese-Americans had lost their property because of unpaid taxes or for other reasons. And many of those who returned home still faced intense hostility from their neighbors.

Despite all this, Japanese-Americans went to fight for the U.S. Some of the soldiers who liberated the German concentration camps had left their families behind in U.S. internment camps. Some of those veterans and other formerly interned citizens later became members of Congress.

Congressional investigations long after the fact concluded that there had been no legitimate national security justification for the internment. In fact, no Japanese-American or Japanese immigrant living in the U.S. at the time was ever convicted of serious acts of espionage or sabotage. In 1988, President Reagan finally apologized to the survivors of the interment camps and restitution was paid. For a long time, the internment of Japanese-Americans was widely regarded as a national shame. Now some commentators attempt to justify those actions and compare them with restrictive measures which some wish to impose on American Muslims.

In peacetime, immigrants have been accused of political extremism and anarchy. Many of the early European immigrants were indeed reformers and radicals. The German-Americans attracted the ire of some of their Anglo neighbors by pushing hard for the abolition of slavery. A significant number of Russian Jewish immigrants and Italian Catholic immigrants had socialist leanings and became active in movements for workers' rights and other social reforms. That legacy is seen as a cause for lament or celebration — depending on the perspective of the historian.

It is also true that a few immigrant reformers and radicals turned to violence. While these represented a tiny fraction of immigrants from their nations, their stories loomed large in the popular imagination and fanned fears of all immigrants.

The 1896 Haymarket bombing, described in the previous chapter, was widely blamed on foreign-born anarchists. Since the actual bomber was never discovered, we don't know whether this claim is accurate.

In 1901, Leon Czolgosz, the son of Polish immigrants, assassinated President William McKinley, and explained later that he did so because, "I done my duty. I didn't believe one man should have so much service and another man should have none."[lvii] Czolgosz had lost his job, had been involved in strikes which were violently suppressed, was sick and may also have been mentally ill. He had spent time in anarchist circles — where many people took him for a government spy due to his extreme awkwardness — but he said, and there was no evidence to disprove, that the assassination was his own idea and not a group effort. Still, many Americans saw his crime as what might be expected from foreign radicals. A sympathetic article by immigrant anarchist Emma Goldman, complained that the violence perpetrated by states and by strike-breakers was never condemned, while the violence of anarchists was called terrorism and did little to help U.S. natives' perceptions of the anarchist cause. In 1903, laws were tightened to prevent the entry of anarchists or radicals.

In 1912, as the previous chapter details, the immigrants and internationalists of the IWW who helped to organize the Bread and Roses strike were accused of fomenting violence. Many Wobblies and strikers were arrested after a cache of dynamite was discovered. They were quietly released again when it turned out that the dynamite had been planted by a relative of the mill owners in order to incriminate the anarchists. When a woman was shot in a clash between strikers and police, two leaders of the Wobblies, (one of them an Italian immigrant), were arrested for incitement of violence. They insisted that they had always preached nonviolence. Their supporters said the woman was shot by police, while their opponents claimed that she was shot by a striker trying to shoot a policeman. In the end, the organizers were found innocent. As with the Haymarket bombing, no one ever found out who had fired the fatal shot.

The First World War only exacerbated the tensions between reformers with Communist tendencies and the U.S. government. As noted before, many of the reformers saw the war as a distraction from the struggle of the laborer for greater freedom. And the Russian Revolution which turned Russia into a Communist state also ended Russia's support for the Allies. Some of the fervor directed against Germans and German-Americans also turned against Communists, Socialists and immigrants in general.

After the war, as some decorated German-Americans returned home, anti-German sentiment gradually subsided but anti-radical sentiment did not.

The American Legion, formed in part to help returning servicemen find work, cope with injuries and shell shock and avoid scams, also became a voice for what they called "100% Americanism" and passed a resolution in favor of the government "immediately deporting every one of those Bolsheviks or IWWs."[lviii] This call fell on sympathetic ears. After red flags were seen in a parade in 1918, *The Washington Post* ran a scathing editorial: "The liberty of the world has just been won at an awful sacrifice of blood and treasure. Shall that liberty be tainted and polluted by the anarchy of bolshevism? Is America to be the scene of activity for soviets and soldiers and workmen's councils, with license for the mob to rob and pillage and with no protection to life and liberty? The activities of crack-brained *radicals and unreconstructed aliens who fail to appreciate the blessings of a free government* must be suppressed..." (Emphasis mine.) It went on to note approvingly that "the board of aldermen of New York has adopted an ordinance prohibiting the display of red flags in parades or public meetings in that city and fixing a maximum penalty of $100 fine and ten days' imprisonment for violation of it. And the New York police are ready with valiant nightsticks to enforce it, backed by 3,000,000 loyal citizens willing to assist ..."[lix]

Many radicals understandably resented this. Some expressed their resentment in scathing speeches and editorials; others in strikes. But a small group expressed their resentments with dynamite. In 1919, a series of bombs were mailed to or detonated at the homes of political leaders who had taken an active part in campaigns against radicals. These were accompanied by leaflets signed by "The Anarchist Fighters:" "We have been dreaming of freedom, we have talked of liberty, we have aspired to a better world and you jailed us, you clubbed us, you deported us, you murdered us whenever you could ... Do not expect us to sit down and pray and cry. We accept your challenge and mean to stick to our war duties. We know that all you do is for your defense as a class; we know also that the proletariat has the same right to protect itself, since their press has been suffocated, their mouths muzzled; we mean to speak for them the voice of dynamite ... [lx]"

Only two people died from those bombings — one of those being a bomb-maker — but the property damage and resulting fear, were great. One of the bombs went off at the home of U.S. Attorney General Mitchell Palmer, who launched a crusade against anarchists. Luigi Galleani, an Italian immigrant and anarchist who had advocated violent protest and published instructions for bomb-making, was deported. That made a certain amount of sense, although no direct link between Galleani and the 1919 bombings had been established. But the lack of such a link drove Palmer to round up and remove more people who might conceivably have been responsible for the explosions.

In November 1919, the police began massive raids on the headquarters of the Russian Workers' Unions and other organizations suspected of radicalism. Large numbers of people were arrested and 559 non-citizen detainees were deported ... not because of any evidence linking them to terrorism but simply because their world view was deemed threatening. Since they were not U.S. citizens, they could be deported on suspicion. There was a great deal of support for the deportations in the popular press. After the USS Buford sailed for Russia with a cargo of deportees, *The Saturday Evening Post* noted approvingly that, "The Mayflower brought the first of the builders to this country; the Buford has taken away the first destroyers."[lxi] "It is hoped and expected," said *The Cleveland Plain Dealer*, "that other vessels larger, more commodious, and carrying similar cargoes, will follow in her wake."[lxii]

Attorney General Palmer had similar hopes. On the night of January 2, 1920, more sweeping surprise raids were conducted by the police, enthusiastically assisted by volunteers from the American Legion, against labor organizations and Communist groups. The dragnet caught a fair number of random people as well, including people picked off the streets for "looking radical" or stopping to ask what was going on.[lxiii] The "seditious materials" collected as evidence included a large hand-lettered sign which said, in Russian, "No Smoking." [lxiv]

The people thus detained were sorted according to citizenship status. U.S. citizens were turned over to state authorities and mostly released for lack of evidence. Non-citizens were marched in chains to detention centers to await processing and probable deportation. Conditions in those centers were brutal. Four hundred people were crammed into an unheated and dirty facility on Deer Island, Mass. Two detainees died of pneumonia, one fell from a fifth-story window and another had a nervous breakdown. Detainees in New York reported being beaten for inexplicable reasons. In some cases, immigrants were questioned in English, which they understood very poorly, and no translator was provided; some of these people were marked down as suspicious and uncooperative.

Public opinion was with Palmer at first. *The Washington Post* declared, "There is no time to waste in hairsplitting over infringement of liberty ..." But when the New York Assembly moved to expel its duly elected members who were Socialists, people of different parties began to feel that the thing had gone too far. Newspaper editors, judges, and congressmen began to argue for the importance of civil liberties. And, as translators were finally brought to deal with detainees, it was found that many of them still did not know why they were being held and most had no obvious connection to radical activity or violence. Palmer tried to rekindle public alarm by claiming a great anarchist attack was planned for May Day. When no attack materialized, his influence waned rapidly.

The final common argument about immigration and national security is based, not on the presumption that immigrants are violent, but on the fact that immigrants are different. According to this argument, nations are held together by ethnic and racial bonds. Small minority populations can be tolerated as non-threatening. But where large groups of people from different ethnic backgrounds try to live together, racial tension inevitably results. "It is precisely in the most diverse societies," Peter Brimelow wrote in his 1995 anti-immigrant manifesto, *Alien Nation,* "that people are most conscious of ethnicity and race. It was in the Austro-Hungarian Empire, where the Germans were a minority exposed to Slavs, Magyars, and Jews from the shtetls of Galicia, that anti-Semitism first became a viable electoral force — and Adolf Hitler spent his formative years."[lxv]   Nor, in his view, are the dangers limited to rising white supremacy. He argues that countries with high rates of ethnic diversity are prone to secession and civil war. He cites examples including the partition of India and Pakistan, the breakoff of Eritrea and the genocidal violence marking the breakup of Yugoslavia.

How does this argument look in the light of U.S. history? It is certainly true that waves of immigration have sometimes been followed by ugly incidents of anti-immigrant violence, as in the violent expulsion of Chinese immigrants on the West Coast, the Know Nothing attacks on German and Irish-Americans, or the lynching of Italians in New Orleans. These actions were reprehensible and deeply disturbing. They did not overturn the American political system or lead to civil war.

It is also worth noting that the two civil wars which have been fought on our nation's soil came *before* most of the great waves of new immigrants and were not fought along ethnic lines. Brimelow himself, arguing that America is not essentially a multicultural society, writes, "*Remember — practically until the Civil War, white Protestants were America.*" [lxvi][Emphasis his] If you define "America" as "most American citizens," he has a point there. And those white Protestants could not agree about how to govern themselves. The American Revolution, and later the Civil War, had white Anglo-Saxon Protestants leading and fighting on both sides. Both wars split families down the middle. Homogeneity, it would appear, is no guarantor of peace.

Chapter Seven

Immigration and Religion

Religious fervor and religious tension have been part of the American experience from the beginning. People of many faiths have come to the U.S. fleeing religious persecution or seeking open spaces or open laws which would permit them to live out their beliefs. Once established, those same people have often looked askance at other true believers coming to put their own versions of a holy life into practice.

The question of immigration also divides members of the same faith from one another. For many Americans, religion is still a basic source of moral guidance and the question of immigration is profoundly moral as well as practical. Does our faith call us to welcome strangers? To separate ourselves from those who may be impure influences? To shape our nation's laws in a way that supports our religious beliefs? To shape our nation's laws in a way that allows freedom for others' religious beliefs? These thorny questions divide members of the same congregations — and may also divide the minds of some individuals.

The first part of this chapter addresses the different faiths which immigrants have brought with them and some of the ways in which these faiths have changed, and been changed by, the American experience.

The second part addresses differing understandings of what faith requires of us. I look at those questions within the context of the Christian community, for two reasons. First, Christianity is the majority religion in the U.S. A 2015 Gallup poll found that 75% of Americans self-identified as Christian, 5% identified with some non-Christian religious faith and 20% were unaffiliated; and most or all our Presidents have identified themselves as Christian.[9] Second, I have spent my life as part of widely varied Christian faith communities and I have some inside understanding of how our disagreements work. I am uncertain of my ability to accurately understand and reflect the conversation within any other religious group.

Faiths of Our Fathers

When the U.S. was still a British colony, many Europeans crossed the Atlantic for religious reasons. In the 1600s, large tracts of New England were settled by Puritans escaping the Anglican domination of England and the growing religious and political tensions which eventually erupted into civil war. The Puritans spoke of establishing "a City on a Hill" in a place where they could live freely as adherents of the true faith. Having settled, they began to disagree sharply with each other about just how this faith should look. Rhode Island was settled under the leadership of Puritan Roger Williams, who had been expelled by his fellow Puritans from Massachusetts and who resolved to allow religious freedom in his jurisdiction.

Other religious nonconformists from England got a less than warm welcome in Massachusetts. Various Catholics, Quakers and Anabaptists were expelled

---

[9] The "most or" qualifier refers to Jefferson, who is described as a Christian by some and a Deist by others, and Lincoln, who was reticent about his religion and is variously identified as a Christian, an atheist or an agnostic by historians.

from there or hanged there. The Quaker William Penn established a settlement in Pennsylvania, also open to people of varied faiths. Maryland was established under Catholic leadership and became a haven for Catholics and other religious minorities. A 1649 law in Maryland forbade the use of religious insults (and included a long and colorful list of forbidden terms.)

England was not the only country sending nonconformists abroad. German Mennonites and other small religious communities left their home states when Lutheranism and Catholicism were declared the only acceptable religions. Many of these emigrants settled in the Midwest and set up their own communities. Others settled on the East Coast. Pennsylvania was a haven for German Anabaptists, Moravians, Schwenkfelders and Dunkers. French Huguenots fleeing their country's religious wars or getting out during periods of Catholic domination, settled along the East Coast.

Some religious emigrants fled, not from explicit religious persecution but from what they saw as a decadent and soul-stifling culture. In the late 1600s, Welsh Quaker John Bevan wrote that his wife greatly desired to move her family to Pennsylvania because it "might be a good place to train up children amongst a sober people and to prevent the corruption of them here by the loose behavior of youths and the bad example of too many of riper years."[lxvii]

Some American settlers were also glad to have freedom from the institutional leaders of their own religions and to settle into a more open-ended form of religious practice. One Norwegian immigrant wrote home, "In America you associate with good and kindly people. Everyone has the freedom to practice the teaching and religion he prefers ... this is Canaan." [That is, the Promised Land.] Another wrote, "We go to the Episcopal or Protestant church which agrees with the Lutheran in practically everything. In fact, we are so happy with the Episcopal church that we don't intend to write to the Norwegian Lutheran church to send us a clergyman. No! There are very few things that we can import from our Old Norway that could be of benefit to us, and least of all Norwegian [church] officials."[lxviii]

Explicit government interference in matters of religion was formally ended by the First Amendment to the U.S. Constitution, though state laws on this point had been relaxing. The details of what this meant were worked out slowly over time. For instance, many states had laws banning certain types of commercial activity on Sunday until the late twentieth century.

Many early European-American communities were initially set up on utopian religious lines, but these rules and identifications tended to weaken over time. Pennsylvania was set up by pacifist Quakers but populated by a wide religious mix including many non-pacifists. As Native Americans began to take up arms on a large scale, pushing back against their dispossession by European immigrants, pressure from the English Crown and from non-pacifist Pennsylvanians mounted. A long series of legal battles and maneuvers throughout the 1700s resulted in volunteer military forces being permitted. One temporary militia law was passed in the 1750s and then went dormant. As the Revolution gathered steam, the American authorities insisted on instituting compulsory military service.

In other cases, the accommodation was casual and gradual. Some German-American utopian communities shed their rules as the second generation took over, becoming farming or industrial communities, which might still be largely though informally, linked by common worship.

Still, religious principles played a strong — and sometimes contradictory — part in the shaping of America. Some claimed that Christianity gave Europeans a right and a mandate to take the land away from its pagan Native inhabitants and claim it for Christ. Others held views similar to the Quaker minister John Woolman, who traveled among the Native Americans to hear what God might have to say to them and returned with a strong sense that God required that they be respected and treated well.

Wars tended to bring God in on both sides. The Declaration of Independence's statement that "We hold these truths to be self-evident, that all men are created equal, that they are endowed by their Creator with certain unalienable Rights ..." is a religious statement, hard to dispute on its own and used in this case to justify secession from England. But there were also preachers who reminded their congregants that rebellion was as the sin of witchcraft and that St Paul had urged submission to the governing authorities. Slavery also was fiercely opposed — and fiercely supported — by people claiming to speak for the same God. And those who agreed that God forbade slavery, disagreed about whether God permitted it to be abolished by violence. The former disagreement cut through the middle of many Christian denominations; the latter tended to pit members of the pacifist denominations against others. The strikes of the 1900s were also fervently praised and fervently disparaged, from both Catholic and Protestant pulpits.

Until the early 1800s, America was largely Protestant. Outside the Catholic haven of Maryland, U.S. Catholics tended to be extremely circumspect in their religious practices, trying to avoid either legal persecution or informal harassment by their neighbors. But the great waves of new European immigration from the 1840s on began to shift the balance toward Catholicism. In 1850, Catholics made up 5% of the U.S. population. By 1906, they were 17% of the population and made up the largest single denomination in the country.[lxix] (This may still seem like a fairly small percentage but bear in mind the present U.S. consternation over how to deal with Muslim immigrants, who made up only 1% of the U.S. population in 2016; currently expected to rise to 2% by 2050.[lxx])

Irish and Italian immigrants were overwhelmingly Catholic, as were many Polish immigrants. One-third of Germans were Catholic. Many of the immigrants worshiped in ethnic churches where the preaching was done in their own languages. Native-born U.S. citizens did not necessarily worship alongside them but the increasingly visible Catholic presence made it easier for native-born Catholics to practice their faith openly. The newcomers also introduced parochial schools, and in some cases, were reluctant to pay taxes to support public schools which their own children did not attend.

This strongly held Catholic identity roused the fears of some American Protestants. Some argued that the Catholics were immigrating in large numbers in the hopes of forming a large enough party to seize political power and subject the U.S. to the authority of the Pope. This accusation and the resulting fear fueled the rise of the American Party (as it called itself), when some of its members came into the open to run for office. The name which stuck to them was "Know Nothings," since the party was reluctant to engage in public debate and would not publish its issue positions or the names of its members. People questioned about their American Party affiliation or about the American Party's beliefs, were instructed to answer, "I know nothing." A surviving copy of their party platform declares "War to the hilt on Political Romanism," and "Hostility to all Papal Influences, when brought to bear against the American Republic," as well as tougher immigration laws, universal public schooling supported by taxes and a ban on foreign-born or Catholic candidates running for office.[lxxi] The American Party reached its political peak in the years shortly before the American Civil War — helped along by instances of anti-immigrant and anti-Catholic vigilantism like those described in Chapter One.

The Civil War ended the relevance of the American Party, but not the popular prejudice against Catholics, particularly immigrant Catholics. Arthur Cleveland Coxe's warning against invading aliens, quoted in Chapter Four, was directed against Irish Catholics, not only because they were Irish, but also because they were Catholic. He wrote, "Look at the city of New York — invaded, seized, and held by aliens who have ... turn[ed] its government into the hands of a religious sect governed by priests ... When a vast number of the ignorant and vicious outcasts of the Latin races, and others, enslaved by hereditary superstition to the dictates of the Roman court, are daily aggregated, but not assimilated, with our people, they become a menace to all that is dear to Americans of the older colonization ... Shall our children's children see another centennial commemoration of Washington and the Constitution? I think every thoughtful man must pronounce such a consummation improbable in the extreme."[lxxii] With a few slight tweaks, the language would suit those alarmists who now declare that the U.S. Constitution is menaced by Muslims owing a secret allegiance to sharia law.

Catholics in the U.S. disagreed among themselves about how best to respond to this hostility. Some Catholics, particularly high-ranking clergy, and particularly the Irish who were the most numerous, pressed for an end to ethnic churches and a unified, Americanized form of Catholicism, urging the faithful to "glory in the title of American citizen."[lxxiii] But members and leaders of many smaller or more recent immigrant faith communities held to the traditions of their own people. Not all Catholics practiced their faith in the same way. First-generation Italian immigrants had a manner of worship more focused on the home and less on the church. They also had a tradition of street festivals honoring saints, which brought their community together and reminded them of home, while drawing the sometimes hostile attention of Protestant neighbors and the exasperation of Catholics wishing to be accepted as completely normal American citizens. The second generation, however, was often more willing to assimilate with Catholics from other countries.

The Catholic presence in the U.S. grew in numbers and in influence. In 2007, nearly one-quarter of the U.S. population was Catholic (that figure has since fallen to one-fifth.) In 2015, 41% of Catholics were members of ethnic minority groups (which no longer included either Irish or Italians, who had become subsumed into the vague category known as "white.") [lxxiv] John Kennedy's election to the presidency was made more difficult, but not stopped, by lingering anti-Catholic prejudices; his time in office served, among other things, to confirm that Catholics really are American. The Supreme Court justices were mainly Protestant for many years, but in 2016, six of the nine sitting justices were Catholic. Few Americans today would argue that this has led to "government by priests," although some advocates of abortion rights believe they would have a better chance if fewer justices were Catholic (though evangelical Protestants are not much more open to their arguments.)

Catholics have played prominent and contradictory roles in the American conversation around ethics and politics. The U.S. bishops have usually spoken against abortion and birth control and for freer immigration. Catholics outside the religious hierarchy have practiced their faith in multifarious ways. Catholicism has been invoked by white supremacist and anti-immigrant celebrities including Father Coughlin, the populist priest and radio broadcaster of the mid-1900s, who justified Kristallnacht and the Nazi persecution as just retribution for the way in which Jews and money lenders had persecuted Christians, and Steve Bannon, President Trump's former advisor whose white supremacist views were discussed in Chapter Four. It also inspired the Kennedys, whose outspoken advocacy for civil rights and immigration reform helped to dismantle many of the legal mechanisms of race discrimination, as well as Dorothy Day and the Catholic Worker movement, which combined Coughlin's concern for economic justice with appeals for equality of all races and care for immigrants. Prominent U.S. Catholics have endorsed just-war theory and invoked it to sanction U.S. wars, while equally prominent U.S. Catholics have endorsed pacifism and protested U.S. wars, sometimes going to prison in the process. Catholicism in the U.S. today seems to be as passionately held and as variegated as Americanism.

Jewish immigrants reached America in several waves. Sephardic Jews from Latin America began to arrive in the New World and settle along the East Coast during the late 1600s. Many of these were merchants and tradesmen looking for new opportunities. In the 1800s, Jews from Germany began to emigrate in large numbers. Some had participated in or sympathized with the pro-democracy uprisings which were quashed; others were escaping from laws which confined them to ghettoes and deprived them of civil rights because of their religion. German-American Jews and Gentiles arrived on the same ships, sometimes settled in the same parts of the country (many in Ohio and other parts of the Midwest) and not infrequently, intermarried. This alliance was strengthened by the fact that some German Jews had helped the Salzburgers, (nonconformist Protestants also fleeing religious persecution,) in their escape from Germany. Salzburgers who settled in America were inclined to offer help to newly settled Jews. Protestant ministers and Jewish rabbis occasionally visited each other's places of worship and preached on themes acceptable to both.

Moving to America did not altogether free Jewish immigrants from the perils of anti-Semitism. The laws said they were free to worship as they would but the press was sometimes hostile. During the Civil War, the Northern press wrote that Northern Jews — members of "the accursed race who killed Christ"— were smuggling gold and supplies to the Confederacy. Seven Jews in the Union Army received Congressional medals of honor but General Grant continued trying to expel all Jews from his department until President Lincoln overruled him. After the war anti-Semitism declined, for a while.

Reform Judaism was first established in Germany but it flowered most fully in the U.S. The first Jewish Reform congregation established in the U.S. in the 1820s, was found too radical by most prospective members and eventually died out. However, many more progressive German Jews immigrated in the mid-1800s and the Reform movement in the U.S. revived and spread rapidly. The Reform movement featured more music, used the vernacular instead of Hebrew, mixed seating of men and women, and scaled back ritual laws; some saw it as a fully Americanized form of Judaism. Others feared that it was too American and not Jewish enough and that the next generation of Jews would lose their identity.

In the 1880s, the third wave of Jewish immigration began. Russian and Polish Jews came fleeing chronic poverty made worse by anti-Jewish laws — also, increasingly, fleeing pogroms. In Russia, the Jews were widely, and unjustly blamed for the chaos that followed Czar Alexander's assassination in 1881. They were also blamed for their perceived role in Communist or Socialist revolutionary organizations demanding social justice. There was indeed an active (and generally nonviolent) Jewish Socialist organization called the Bund, containing by some estimates, 10% of Russia's Jews. But all Jews were equally at risk from government-encouraged mob violence and many determined to escape. Between 1881 and 1914, approximately two million Jews emigrated to the U.S. The tumults of the First World War and the Russian Revolution displaced even more.

These Jewish immigrants often arrived with little or no money. They settled along the East Coast and took low-wage industrial jobs; some became very active in the labor movement. They strove to give their children better opportunities and indeed, the second generation made great strides in education.

The poverty of the early immigrants and the success of their children were both resented by some in the New World. Chapter Four discussed the ways in which poorer Jewish immigrants were stigmatized as squalid and subhuman, and more successful arrivals as grasping and menacing. These sentiments, echoed by such celebrity figures as Henry Ford and Father Coughlin, may have contributed to the U.S.'s unwillingness to receive Jewish refugees as the Nazis rose to power. Some described reports of Nazi atrocities as obvious lies and propaganda being promulgated by Jews trying to advance some sinister agenda of their own.

The aftermath of the war changed American attitudes, at least for a while. The soldiers who had liberated the concentration camps were all too aware that the reports of Nazi atrocities had been genuine. One hundred and forty thousand survivors of the camps arrived in the U.S. after the passage of the 1948 Displaced Persons Act. Many of these immigrants were much more orthodox in their Judaism than the Sephardic or German immigrants had been. This was not so with the next wave of Jews who came from the Soviet Union, where religious observance had largely been forced underground.

In 2013, about 2% of the U.S. population identified themselves as Jews, with most of these using the term in a religious as well as an ethnic sense[lxxv]. In 2016, one-third of the U.S. Supreme Court Justices were Jewish. Jewish-American influence on American art, music, literature and film has been profound. So has Jewish influence on U.S. politics and ethics — though this had been, like Catholic influence, widely varied. Jewish-Americans have taken prominent roles in the labor movement and in a wide range of civil rights movements. Recently, many of them have spoken strongly against anti-Muslim prejudice in the U.S. These activities tend to fall on the liberal end of the U.S. political spectrum. On the other hand, political support for Israel, (also widespread among American Jews), is more often seen as a politically conservative trait. Overall, Jews in the U.S. are more likely to be Democrats than Republicans, but the Orthodox are far more likely to be Republican.[lxxvi]

Muslim immigration to the U.S. is not an entirely new phenomenon. The first large wave of Muslim immigrants was not voluntary; they were enslaved Africans brought to the Colonies — and later the United States — against their will. Historians have estimated that one-fourth to one-third of this population may have been Muslim.

In the early 1900s, voluntary Muslim immigrants began to arrive along with Arab Christians. Many of these Muslim immigrants clustered and settled together in the Midwest. The first mosque in the nation was built in 1920. The 1921 immigration quota system effectively barred Muslims.

The next growth in American Islam came — not from immigrants — but from African-Americans moving north in the Great Migration between and after the World Wars; looking for the faith of their forefathers. Today, about one-third of Muslims in the U.S. are African-American.

The reforms of the 1960s made Muslim immigration possible again from the Persian Gulf, Northern Africa and Southeast Asia. Muslims from very different cultures and schools of thought arrived together in the U.S. and handled the adjustment process in varied ways. Their numbers were small, and they began to arrive in a period when U.S. popular culture was inclined to celebrate diversity--although during U.S. involvement in the Gulf War in the 1990s, there was some generalized anti-Arab sentiment which rapidly spread to become anti-Muslim sentiment. This escalated rapidly in the wake of the September 11 terror attacks. Too many people remembered that the attackers had been Muslim and forgot that some of the first responders who risked their lives to rescue people on that day were Muslim as well. President Bush reminded the nation of the latter fact and called on Americans to avoid anti-Muslim prejudice. He also authorized surveillance programs which were widely perceived as relying on religious and racial profiling. The years since then have seen an increase in hostility towards Muslims in some circles, exacerbated by the rise of the present administration. They have also seen increasing Muslim involvement in the U.S. political system. U.S. Representative Keith Ellison of Minnesota, elected in 2006, became the first Muslim in the U.S. Congress.

What Does the Lord Require of Us?

American Christians (the majority of U.S. voters), have been and still are deeply divided over how their faith should affect their stance on immigration. Both sides quote the Scriptures liberally in support of their positions.

In 1882, George Frisbie Hoar, a Republican senator, was one of the few U.S. statesmen willing to oppose the Chinese Exclusion Act. He reminded his listeners that the Declaration of Independence stated that all men were endowed by their Creator with inalienable rights, including the pursuit of happiness and that this meant governments had no right to interfere with any person's choice "to go everywhere on the surface of the earth that his welfare may require," and he went on to quote, "He made of one blood all nations of men to dwell on the face of the earth." He saw in this statement the condemnation of Chinese exclusion and all other manifestations of "the old race prejudice which has so often played its hateful and bloody part in history."[lxxvii]

Arthur Cleveland Coxe was warier about this. "In the spirit of Christianity itself," he said, "it is true our just laws admit to our civil and social rights, Jews, Turks, infidels and pagans of all professions; but surely not with any idea that such large and liberal dealings are, in themselves, a subversion of our Christianity and a proclamation that our moral and social system is extinguished in concessions to minorities..."[lxxviii] He went on to explain that any sort of Catholic influence on government was an obvious breach of our moral and social systems.

The same arguments continue to the present day. Advocates for immigrants are apt to quote such Old Testament verses as "The stranger that dwelleth among you shall be unto you as one born among you and you shall love him well; for ye were strangers in the land of Egypt."[lxxix] (Leviticus 19:34), or, "I will be a swift witness against the sorcerers and against the adulterers and against those who swear falsely and against those who oppress the wage earner in his wages, the widow and the orphan and those who turn aside the alien, and do not fear Me," says the LORD of hosts." (Malachi 3:5b)[lxxx]

Peter Brimelow, in his anti-immigrant manifesto, suggests that Christians ought to pay equal attention to another Old Testament text: "The stranger that is within thee shall get above thee very high; and thou shalt come down very low. He shall lend to thee and thou shalt not lend to him; he shall be the head and thou shalt be the tail." (Deuteronomy 28:43-44)[lxxxi] This argument may be somewhat weakened by considering the context; this threat is given, not as a consequence of allowing aliens in but as a punishment from God which will be incurred if the Israelites disobey God's laws. But there are other texts in the Old Testament which warn against following foreign gods and which can be expanded into arguments against allowing members of other religions to influence U.S. government policy. Of course, this argument comes close to advocating a theocratic system, which the Constitution is generally understood to avoid. There are certainly passages about the importance of upholding the laws, which tend to be cited by those who favor a crackdown on illegal immigration, as well as stories whose heroes break the law of the land in the interest of following God's law, which tend to be cited by those on the other side. This part of the argument says nothing about how restrictive immigration laws should be.

Some Christians hold that welcoming refugees at least, and probably other immigrants, is required by the basic law set out in Leviticus and confirmed as of primary importance in the Gospels: "Love your neighbor as yourself."[lxxxii] This, of course, raises what may be the most fundamental question in the immigration debate: Who is my neighbor?

Brimelow makes it clear that he believes it's impossible to treat everyone equally as neighbors. He quotes Proudhon as saying, "If all the world is my brother, then I have no brother," and goes on to say, "This is a succinct statement of the impossibility of rational and meaningful moral action if our responsibilities are viewed as limitless — the condition that Garret Hardin calls 'promiscuous altruism.' The only way to navigate in the sea of human pain is to make distinctions. The moral market will fail unless some equivalent of property lines is specified. Our rights and duties have to be put in some sort of priority ... Any general moral obligation to minister to strangers is met, and more than matched, by the specific and even stronger moral obligation to protect our own family."[lxxxiii] (This position has some Biblical backing; 1 Timothy 5:8 states that "But if anyone does not provide for his own and especially for those of his household, he has denied the faith and is worse than an unbeliever."[lxxxiv])

Some immigration advocates argue that the U.S. has a specific moral obligation to welcome people from countries which have suffered from U.S. military intervention or which have sent much of their wealth to the U.S. — thanks to globalization.

More broadly, the question of neighborliness is raised in the Gospels as well.

77

Jesus answers it by telling the story of the Good Samaritan — a foreigner of a very unpopular type who rescues a grievously wounded Jew — and urging his hearers to practice this type of mercy.

Faith-based answers may be authoritative for individual believers but they are not the basis of U.S. national policy. The previous section has addressed the question of what it means to be a Christian. The final section addresses the question of what it means to be an American.

What Is America?

Many U.S. citizens (like citizens of most other countries) have cherished the idea that theirs is a superior and singularly blessed nation. They have differed with each other about just what those blessings are. This difference has profound implications for immigration policy.

One school has held that America's identity is based on the cohesion that comes from shared ethnic, cultural and religious traditions.

In the 1787 *Federalist Papers*, Founder John Jay described the new nation as "one united people — a people descended from the same ancestors, speaking the same language, professing the same religion, attached to the same principles of government, very similar in their manners and customs ... a band of brethren."[lxxxv] Alexander Hamilton, Jay's fellow Federalist, explained how this idea of a nation as a homogenous community must shape immigration policy: "The safety of a republic depends essentially on the energy of a common national sentiment; on a uniformity of principles and habits; on the exemption of the citizens from foreign bias and prejudice; and on the love of country which will almost invariably be found to be closely connected with birth, education and family ... foreigners will generally be apt to bring with them attachments to the persons they have left behind; to the country of their nativity and to its particular customs and manners ...The influx of foreigners must, therefore, tend to produce a heterogeneous compound; to change and corrupt the national spirit; to complicate and confound public opinion."[lxxxvi] He felt no need to explain why change and complexity must necessarily be corrupting.

In the mid-1800s, the Know Nothings extolled America as "peerless in strength and beauty, the pride and excellence of the whole earth,"[lxxxvii] and urged, "America for Americans, we say. And why not? Didn't they plant it and battle for it through bloody revolution? Why shouldn't they shape and rule the destinies of their own land — the land red and rich with the blood and ashes, and hallowed with the memories of their fathers? ... Particularly when the alien betrays the trust that should never have been given to him?"[lxxxviii]

In 1924, a Southern Democratic senator spoke in support of the quota laws: "We have in America perhaps the largest percentage of the pure, unadulterated Anglo-Saxon stock ... I would make this not an asylum for the oppressed of all countries but a country to assimilate and perfect that splendid type of manhood."[lxxxix] At the time he spoke for the majority.

By 1965, the tide had turned, but there was still vocal opposition to increasing the diversity of our 'band of brethren." The President of the Daughters of the American Revolution testified before Congress that eliminating the quota system might lead to "a collapse of moral and spiritual values if unassimilable aliens of dissimilar ethnic background and culture are permitted gradually to overwhelm our country."

The same idea appears in present-day Congressman Steve King's remarks, quoted in Chapter Four, about the impossibility of building our civilization with somebody else's babies.

Some people, including prominent members of King's own party, condemned his remarks as un-American. Plainly, he spoke from within one long-established tradition of American thought and political discourse. But there is another equally long-established tradition which prizes equality and diversity more than ethnic homogeneity.

As the U.S. declared independence it asserted that all men were created equal and endowed by their Creator with certain inalienable rights. As mentioned in Chapter One, the nation's first President endorsed a broad vision of humanity and of America in at least some of his public statements, as when he told Irish immigrants that, "the bosom of America is open to receive not only the opulent and respectable stranger but the oppressed and persecuted of all nations."[xc] There were always reservations in how the government actually interpreted the principle of equality and there were always Americans who felt that these reservations undermined the integrity of the government. Abraham Lincoln wrote to a friend in 1855, "As a nation we began by declaring that 'all men are created equal.' We now practically read it 'all men are created equal, except Negroes.' When the Know-Nothings get control, it will read 'all men are created equal, except Negroes and foreigners and Catholics'."[xci]

During the time of the immigration quotas, a vocal minority of statesmen continued to uphold a different vision, both of immigrants and of America. Emanuel Celler, Senator and persistent advocate of an open immigration policy, wrote in his 1953 autobiography (published while real reform still seemed a distant prospect), "There were men older than I in Congress, men of more experience, of more learning. Yet the talk … did not fit into the picture I knew. I knew the women in the Brooklyn tenements who scrubbed their floors again and again in the helpless fight against squalor. I knew the timid, perplexed son of the immigrant — part of him Old World, part of him New —serious and hungry, filling the free schools and the free colleges of New York. I knew the Negro, kept down in poverty and degradation. The folklore of Poland, of Lithuania, of Russia, of Italy, became part of my folklore because I had heard it so often. I knew their richness and their laughter and the disappointing heartbreak of the struggle in America to adjust. I knew, also, their pride; the unfulfilled dream of independence that had first brought them here."[xcii] For him, the shared dream of independence was all-important and the diversity of culture an enrichment instead of a threat.

During this same period the man who became John Kennedy's grandfather, Congressman John Fitzgerald, recalls having this dialogue with Senator Henry Cabot Lodge:

Lodge: "You are an impudent young man. Do you think the Jews or Italians have any right in this country?"

Fitzgerald: "As much right as your father or mine. It was only a difference of a few ships."[xciii]

The Second World War gave added impetus to this inclusive vision. In 1944, Swedish historian Gunnar Myrdal wrote, "Fascism and Nazism are based on a racial superiority dogma — not unlike the old hackneyed American caste theory — and they came to power by means of racial persecution and oppression. Therefore, Americans must stand before the whole world in support of racial tolerance and equality ... When in this crucial time, the international leadership passes to America, the great reason for hope is that this country has a national experience of uniting racial and cultural diversities and a national theory, if not a consistent practice, of freedom and equality for all ..." [xciv]

One year earlier, signing an order which created the only all-Japanese American combat unit in the war, Franklin Delano Roosevelt had said that "The principle on which this country was founded and by which it has always been governed, is that Americanism is a matter of mind and heart. Americanism is not, and never was, a matter of race or ancestry."[xcv] He said this at a time when thousands of Japanese-Americans were still being interned — for no other reason than their ancestry — under his authority. This perhaps underscored Myrdal's point about the gap between national theory and practice.

John Kennedy promised to work to make the vision FDR had described a practical reality and after Kennedy was killed, President Johnson carried on the work of immigration reform. In his first State of the Union speech, he described his vision of a world "in which all men, goods and ideas can freely move across every border and every boundary ..." and said that, "A nation that was built by the immigrants of all lands can ask those who now seek admission: 'What can you do for our country?' But we should not be asking, 'In what country were you born?'"[xcvi]

Soon laws were passed to make the second part of his vision a reality. The first part has not yet come true but some voices still speak up for it.

Both sides of the immigration debate, then, can claim with some validity to represent "American values" and the vision of the Founders and of later great statesmen and thinkers. The question of immigration cannot be settled by anything so simple as an appeal to history. Nor is there agreement about how much of our country's history calls us to pride and fidelity; how much to repentance and restitution. What, then, of a more pragmatic approach?

It is clearly true that creating national unity across lines of ethnicity is not easy. Things can go wrong on several levels.

Cultural differences about whether eye contact is considered friendly or rude, or about how close people stand when speaking, or about what questions are considered too personal, can lead to personal conflicts. Such conflicts have often been passed by word of mouth from neighbor to neighbor and escalated into community-wide tensions. In the age of social media, such stories can be decontextualized, exaggerated and spread nationwide among groups of like-minded people almost instantly.

More serious ethical differences may also be culturally inflected. How should we balance protection of free speech with protection of people who may be harmed by speech that is fraudulent or inflammatory? How should we balance the right to practice one's religion freely with the right not to be oppressed by someone else's religion? The answers have never been easy.

Of course, these serious ethical differences exist within each ethnic group as well as between them. Plenty of white American families with no recent immigrant ancestry now find it difficult to speak to one another in the wake of our last divisive election. Nor is the diversity of opinion which now exists entirely the result of a too-diverse society. In the days of the Founders, which both Arthur Cleveland Coxe and Peter Brimelow looked back to as a glorious time of harmony and homogeneity, the U.S. had just come through a bloody civil war fought largely between Anglo-Americans and even the victors could not agree on how to frame the government which they had just won the right to create. Alexander Hamilton, who praised the "common national sentiment ... uniformity of principles and habits ... [and] love of country which will almost invariably be found to be closely connected with birth, education and family," was born in the U.S. to parents of mostly British ancestry and given a high-quality U.S. education. He was killed in a duel with a well-educated U.S.-born child of U.S.-born parents of British ancestry.

Perhaps the challenge and the gift of a more diverse nation lies in the fact that our differences were out in the open from the beginning — that we knew that we may not understand each other and that we may disagree profoundly.

An article published in *Scientific American* in 2014 looks at the results of this knowledge. The authors allow that, "Research has shown that social diversity in a group can cause discomfort, rougher interactions, a lack of trust, greater perceived interpersonal conflict, lower communication, less cohesion, more concern about disrespect and other problems. So, what is the upside?"

The upside, according to them, is substantial. They cited some studies showing better financial results for companies with more ethnic and gender diversity at high levels. Then they described smaller experiments designed to determine why this works. Small groups of subjects were given problem-solving exercises. Each participant had some time to look at information alone; each participant's information contained some unique clues not given ahead of time to other group members. In all-white groups, participants tended to assume (incorrectly) that they all started out with the same information. In racially diverse groups participants were more likely to ask each other, "What do you know?"— and to arrive more quickly at the correct solution. The researchers wrote, "Being with similar others leads us to think we all hold the same information and share the same perspective. This perspective, which stopped the all-white groups from effectively processing the information, is what hinders creativity and innovation."[xcvii]

Extrapolation from carefully controlled research conditions to actual life can be confusing. But there are some real-world stories that harmonize with the researchers' conclusions. In his book, *Nation of Nations,* Tom Gjelten describes several immigrant families struggling to find their place in the U.S. For many of those who immigrated as adults, it was initially difficult to understand or to trust people of a different ethnicity and culture. But some of those adults and many of their children ended up developing friendships and a strong sense of solidarity across ethnic lines with other immigrants from very different cultures. They shared the difficult balance of holding onto the strengths of their home cultures and taking on the best parts of U.S. culture. They shared the challenge of homesickness and of dealing with prejudice from longer-established neighbors. And, they shared a willingness to go out to meet people profoundly different from themselves.

Such solidarity could be seen as a force in opposition to native-born Anglo-Americans. But in this fragmented and alienated culture, most of us, at least sometimes, feel like outsiders and have reason to be grateful for the kindness of strangers.

This has been my experience. As I said in the introduction, I'm an Anglo-American with no recent immigrant ancestry. I work at a small nonprofit farm which frequently hosts long-term guests. Some of our Anglo guests find us disconcerting because we don't altogether fit their picture of what normal Anglo-Americans are supposed to be like. (You eat *beans*? What, no TV? *No TV anywhere*? Are you *serious*?) Many of them have been gracious enough to stick it out, have been good help and good company and have found something here that they were looking for — but there is usually a difficult initial period of adjustment. Our international guests are prepared to find us foreign and are more apt to be pleasantly surprised by and to celebrate the things that we do have in common. And, while I have spent most of my life in small towns, I have sometimes had occasion to visit large cities. When I do this, I tend to get seriously lost, on foot, alone, and depend on strangers to give me directions. Most people look past me and keep on going. Very often the ones who do stop and help me figure out where to go, give their directions in broken English.

Scholar Robert Putnam has observed the same process writ large. He describes the initial challenges of assimilation; the ways in which diversity can lead to hostility, mistrust, and alienation as each group wonders why the other can't see the light and learn to accept their own cultural rules. He also writes about the deeper and richer solidarity which is forged across, rather than within, the boundaries that divide our comfort zones. "The challenge," he writes, "is best met not by making 'them' like 'us,' but rather by creating a newer, more capacious sense of 'we.'"[xcviii]

One last thing before you go. How awesome would it be if you shared your opinion about this book with a short review on Amazon? You read reviews yourself so why not give back a little to the community.

http://booksfor.review/warywelcome

Suggestions for Further Reading:

Ronald Takaki's *A Different Mirror: A History of Multicultural America* (Boston, Little, Brown & Co, 1993) tells the story of the U.S. from the perspective of many different immigrant and minority groups. It's full of quotations from primary sources with very different perspectives.

Tom Gjelten's *A Nation of Nations* (New York, Simon and Schuster, 2015) tells the story of several families of relatively recent immigrants from different cultures settling into the U.S. The middle section of the book takes an in-depth look at the passage of the 1965 immigration reform act which ended the national quota system — and at the attitudes and policies which produced the quota system in the first place.

I highly recommend both these books as starting points for people interested in learning more about U.S. immigration, both historic and contemporary. Several other books also helped me with particular aspects of research.

Jenna Weissman Joselit's *Immigration and American Religion* (Oxford University Press, 2001) describes the successive waves of religious immigration to the U.S. — first nonconforming Protestant, then Catholic, Jewish, Buddhist and Muslim — and the ways in which those faiths shaped and were shaped by American culture.

Vincent J Cannato's *American Passage*, (Harper Collins, 2009) offers an in-depth look at the Atlantic migration and the laws which shaped it.

Peter Brimelow's *Alien Nation: Common Sense About America's Immigration Disaster*, (New York, Random House, 1995) laid out many of the anti-immigration arguments which I had heard from neighbors and media figures, plus a few new ones I hadn't encountered, in a reasonably coherent and highly readable form. I found his arguments unconvincing but was grateful for the chance to understand them better.

The online collections of primary source material maintained by various universities and by the U.S. Congress provided invaluable background and details.

Win a free

kindle
OASIS

Let us know what you thought of this book to enter the sweepstake at:

booksfor.review/warywelcome

About the Author

Joanna Michal Hoyt is an autodidact who has always been fascinated by the rich and contradictory layers of U.S. history revealed in primary sources. She lives and works on a sustainable farm/nonprofit organization/intentional community in rural upstate New York. Many of her neighbors are conservative white folks whose families have been in the U.S. for several generations. Many of her community's guests are immigrants or international visitors. Listening to their varied perspectives on immigration rekindled her interest in America's longstanding ambivalence on this issue.

Joanna writes essays as well as speculative and historical fiction. Her short story "Cracked Reflections," focused on immigration issues during the First World War and the First Red Scare, appeared in the *Mysterion* anthology of Christian speculative fiction. A novel featuring the same main characters is in the works. For more information and links to other stories and essays see www.joannahoyt.blogspot.com

Endnotes

Chapter One:

[i] Graham, Otis L., "Unguarded Gates," Lanham: Rowman and Littlefield, 2004, p. 4

[ii] Cited at ushistory.org, *U.S. History Online Textbook, 2017,* http://www.ushistory.org/us/19e.asp

[iii] Ronald Takaki, A Different Mirror: A History of Multicultural America, Boston, Little, Brown & Co, 1993

Chapter Two:

[iv] Daily Alta California, May 12, 1952, quoted in Ronald Takaki, *A Different Mirror: A History of Multicultural America,* Boston, Little, Brown & Co, 1993, p. 195

[v] Takaki, *A Different Mirror*, p. 174

[vi] Takaki, *A Different Mirror*, p. 178

Chapter Three:

[vii] Reporting and estimates from historian and former CA state senator Joseph Dunn Reported in Alex Wagner, March 6, 2017, "America's Forgotten History of Illegal Deportations," *The Atlantic*: retrieved from https://www.theatlantic.com/politics/archive/2017/03/americas-brutal-forgotten-history-of-illegal-deportations/517971/?utm_source=atlfb

[viii] *Depression, War and Civil Rights: Hispanics in the Southwest,* retrieved from the History, Art and Archives site of the U.S. House of Representatives,

http://history.house.gov/Exhibitions-and-Publications/HAIC/Historical-Essays/Separate-Interests/Depression-War-Civil-Rights/

Chapter Four:

[ix] A. Cleveland Coxe, "Government by Aliens," *Forum*, 1888

[x] Alex Wagner, March 14, 2017, "Steve King Thinks I'm A Threat to American Civilization," *The Atlantic*, https://www.theatlantic.com/politics/archive/2017/03/steve-king-thinks-im-a-threat-to-american-civilization/519399/?utm_source=atlfb

[xi] Ronald Takaki, "A Different Mirror: A History of Multicultural America," Boston, Little, Brown & Co, 1993, p. 280

[xii] U.S. Immigration Commission, "Dictionary of Races or Peoples," 61st Congress, 3rd Session, Document #602; quoted in Tom Gjelten's *A Nation of Nations*, New York, Simon and Schuster, 2015, p. 85

[xiii] Emanuel Celler, "No Choice in Immigrants," letter to the editor, New York Times, July 6, 1923; quoted in Gjelten, *Nation of Nations*, p. 88

[xiv] *Depression, War and Civil Rights: Hispanics in the Southwest*, retrieved from the History, Art and Archives site of the U.S. House of Representatives, http://history.house.gov/Exhibitions-and-Publications/HAIC/Historical-Essays/Separate-Interests/Depression-War-Civil-Rights/

[xv] Senate Report No. 1515, 81st Congress, 2nd Session, 1950,455; quoted in Gjelten, *Nation of Nations* p. 92

[xvi] Remarks at the Signing of the Immigration Bill, October 3, 1965; quoted in Gjelten, *Nation of Nations* p. 132

[xvii] Oral History of Roger Conner, Otis Graham Jr. Papers; quoted in Gjelten, *Nation of Nations* p. 249

[xviii] Takaki, A Different Mirror, p.321

[xix] Robinson, Henry, 'Our Manufacturing Era', Overland Monthly, March 1869 [in Takaki, *A Different Mirror*, p 204]

[xx] Takaki, A Different Mirror, p 331.

[xxi] Henry F. Osborne, quoted in Steven A. Farber, December 2008, "U.S. Scientists' Role in the Eugenics Movement (1907-1939): A Contemporary Biologist's Perspective", in Zebrafish, retrieved from https://www.ncbi.nlm.nih.gov/pmc/articles/PMC2757926/

[xxii] Quoted in Lisa Ko, January 29, 2016, "Unwanted Sterilization and Eugenics Programs in the United States," retrieved from http://www.pbs.org/independentlens/blog/unwanted-sterilization-and-eugenics-programs-in-the-united-states/

[xxiii] Francis A Walker, 'Immigration and Degradation,' *Forum*, August 1891, quoted in Vincent J Cannato, "American Passage," Harper Collins, 2009

[xxiv] William Coates, 'Regulation and to Amend the Naturalization Laws," House Report, 51st Congress, 2nd Session, Report #308, quoted in Cannato, *American Passage*

[xxv] Takaki, A Different Mirror, p.308

[xxvi] Takaki, A Different Mirror, p.306

[xxvii] Ray Stannard Baker, "Human Nature In Hawaii: How the Few Want the Many to Work for Them — Perpetually, and At Low Wages," *American Magazine*, vol 73, January 1912, quoted in Takaki, *A Different Mirror*, p. 264

[xxviii] Rafael Bernal, March 19, 2017, "Reports find that immigrants commit less crime than U.S.-born citizens," *The Hill*, retrieved from http://thehill.com/latino/324607-reports-find-that-immigrants-commit-less-crime-than-us-born-citizens

[xxix] Katie McHugh, July 1, 2015, ""Donald Trump's Criticisms of Mass Mexican Immigration Barely Scratch the Surface," *Breitbart Connect*, retrieved from https://web.archive.org/web/20161117043802/http://www.breitbart.com/

big-government/2015/07/01/donald-trumps-criticisms-of-mass-mexican-immigration-barely-scratch-the-surface/

xxx For one egregious example, see "They Wait For Us," http://www.encyclopedia.com/history/dictionaries-thesauruses-pictures-and-press-releases/national-songs-ballads-and-other-patriotic-poetry-chiefly-relating-war-1846-1846-compiled-william

xxxi Takaki, *A Different Mirror*, p. 327

xxxii Takaki, *A Different Mirror*, p. 306

xxxiii Oscar Handlin, 'The Immigration Fight Has Only Begun,' *Commentary*, July 1, 1952; quoted in Tom Gjelten's "A Nation of Nations," p.100

Chapter Five:

xxxiv Stephen A. Camarota, September 2015, "Welfare Use by Legal and Illegal Immigrant Households," retrieved from http://cis.org/Welfare-Use-Legal-Illegal-Immigrant-Households

xxxv Laura Reston, September 3, 2015, "Immigrants Don't Drain Welfare. They Fund It," retrieved from https://newrepublic.com/article/122714/immigrants-dont-drain-welfare-they-fund-it

xxxvi Felice J. Freyer, March 6, 2017, "Doctors from Banned Countries Serve Millions of Americans, Analysis Finds," Boston Globe: retrieved from https://www.bostonglobe.com/metro/2017/03/06/doctors-from-banned-countries-serve-millions-americans-analysis-finds/wqvN01IEORXh6ZduHydQrL/story.html

xxxvii Steven F. Hipple, "Self-Employment in the United States," Monthly Labor Review, Bureau of Labor Statistics, September 2010,24; quoted in Tom Gjelten's *A Nation of Nations*, New York, Simon and Schuster, 2015, p. 229

xxxviii Then and Now: America's New Immigrant Entrepreneurs, quoted in Tom Gjelten, *Nation of Nations*, p.230

xxxix Ronald Takaki, *A Different Mirror: A History of Multicultural America*, Boston, Little, Brown & Co, 1993, p. 187

xl Takaki, *Different Mirror*, p. 253

xli Cited in *History of Labor in Hawai'i*, from the Center for Labor Education and Research at the University of Hawai'i—West Oahu, retrieved from https://www.hawaii.edu/uhwo/clear/home/HawaiiLaborHistory.html

xlii Cited in *History of Labor in Hawai'i*, retrieved from https://www.hawaii.edu/uhwo/clear/home/HawaiiLaborHistory.html

xliii from The Samuel Gompers Papers Project at the University of Maryland, retrieved from http://www.gompers.umd.edu/AFL%20preamble.htm

xliv Testimony, U.S. Congress, House Select Committee, Sept. 11, 1913, retrieved from the Samuel Gompers Papers Project at the University of Maryland, http://www.gompers.umd.edu/quotes.htm

xlv Samuel Gompers, Testimony, U.S. Congress, Senate Committee on Education and Labor, Aug. 16, 1883; Samuel Gompers to L. W. Tilden, Sept. 16, 1905; Samuel Gompers to William Gerber, May 31, 1923; retrieved from the Samuel Gompers Papers Project at the University of Maryland,

http://www.gompers.umd.edu/quotes.htm#IMMIGRATION

xlvi Takaki, *Different Mirror*, p.188

xlvii Preamble to the IWW Constitution, retrieved from image on http://www.iww.org/culture/official/preamble.shtml

xlviii Boston Globe, January 13, 1912, quoted in Bruce Watson, *Bread and Roses: Mills Migrants and the Struggle for the American Dream*, Penguin, 2006

[xlix] Quoted in Joyce Kornbluh, *Bread and Roses: The 1912 Lawrence textile strike,* retrieved from http://flag.blackened.net/lpp/iww/kornbluh_bread_roses.html

[l] Lawrence Citizens Association, Reign of Terror in an American City, quoted in Watson, *Bread and Roses*

Chapter Six:

[li] Brand Whitlock, *Belgium: A Personal Narrative*, quoted in *World War I: A History in Documents,* edited by Frans Coetzee and Marilyn Shevin-Coetzee, Oxford University Press, 2002, page 95

[lii] Aaron Delwiche, August 22, 2009, *Of Fraud and Force Fast Woven: Domestic Propaganda during the First World War*, retrieved from http://www.firstworldwar.com/features/propaganda.htm

[liii] Daniel A. Gross, July 28, 2014, "The U.S. Confiscated Half A Billion Dollars In Private Property During World War II," *Smithsonian Magazine*, retrieved from http://www.smithsonianmag.com/history/us-confiscated-half-billion-dollars-private-property-during-wwi-180952144/#ixhJvT3uCV51JL4I.99

[liv] T.A. Frail, January 2017, "The Injustice of Japanese-American Internment Camps Resonates Strongly To This Day," in Smithsonian Magazine, retrieved from http://www.smithsonianmag.com/history/injustice-japanese-americans-internment-camps-resonates-strongly-180961422/

[lv] Quoted Ronald Takaki, *A Different Mirror: A History of Multicultural America*, Boston, Little, Brown & Co, 1993, p 380

[lvi] Takaki, *Different Mirror*, p 379

[lvii] "The Legal Aftermath of the Assassination of William McKinley," retrieved from the University of Buffalo Digital Collection, http://library.buffalo.edu/pan-am/exposition/law/

[lviii] Richard Slotkin, Lost Battalions: The Great War and the Crisis of American Nationality, New York: Henry Holt, 2005, p.434

[lix] "Down with the Red Flag," editorial in Washington Post, November 28, 1918; reprinted in "Reds and Americans," a primary source compilation by the National Humanities Center

[lx] Quoted in "Attorney General A. Mitchell Palmer on Charges Made Against Department of Justice by Louis F. Post and Others: Hearings Before the Committee on Rules, House of Representatives, Sixty-sixth Congress, Second Session, Part 1," U.S. Government Printing Office, 1920, p. 165

[lxi] "Sanctuary," Saturday Evening Post, February 7, 1920; quoted in Robert K Murray, *Red Scare: A Study in National Hysteria, 1919-1920*, New York: McGraw-Hill, p. 208

[lxii] Cleveland Plain Dealer, December 23, 1919, p 10, quoted in Murray, *Red Scare*, p. 209

[lxiii] Murray, *Red Scare*, p 213

[lxiv] Roberta S. Feuerlicht, America's Reign of Terror: World War I, the Red scare, and the Palmer raids, New York, Random House, 1971

[lxv] Peter Brimelow, Alien Nation: Common Sense About America's Immigration Disaster, New York, Random House, 1995, p.120

[lxvi] Brimelow, *Alien Nation*, p. 197

Chapter Seven:

[lxvii] Quoted in Jenna Weissman Joselit's *Immigration and American Religion*, Oxford University Press, 2001, page 26

[lxviii] Quoted in Joselit, Immigration and American Religion, pp 38-39

[lxix] Julie Byrne, "Roman Catholics and Immigration in Nineteenth-Century America," retrieved from the National Humanities Center's Teacher Service,

http://nationalhumanitiescenter.org/tserve/nineteen/nkeyinfo/nromcath.htm

lxx Besheer Mohammed, January 6, 2016, "A New Estimate of the U.S. Muslim Population," retrieved from http://www.pewresearch.org/fact-tank/2016/01/06/a-new-estimate-of-the-u-s-muslim-population/

lxxi http://library.duke.edu/rubenstein/scriptorium/americavotes/know-nothing-letter.jpeg

lxxii A. Cleveland Coxe, "Government by Aliens," *Forum*, 1888

lxxiii James Cardinal Gibbons, 1891, quoted in Joselit, "Immigration and American Religion," p. 51

lxxiv "America's Changing Religious Landscape, May 12, 2015 Pew Research Center, retrieved from http://www.pewforum.org/2015/05/12/americas-changing-religious-landscape/

lxxv "A Portrait of Jewish Americans," October 1, 2013, Pew Research Center, retrieved from http://www.pewforum.org/2013/10/01/chapter-1-population-estimates/

lxxvi A Portrait of Jewish Americans," October 1, 2013, Pew Research Center, retrieved from http://www.pewforum.org/2013/10/01/jewish-american-beliefs-attitudes-culture-survey/

lxxvii Charles Frisbie Hoar, Speech on the floor of the U.S. Senate, February 28, 1882, quoted in Tom Gjelten, *A Nation of Nations*, New York, Simon and Schuster, 2015, p 84

lxxviii A. Cleveland Coxe, *Government by Aliens*, 1888

lxxix King James Bible, 2000

lxxx New American Standard Bible, 1977

lxxxi King James Bible, as quoted in Peter Brimelow, *Alien Nation*, Random House, New York, 1995, p 243

lxxxii Leviticus 19:19

[lxxxiii] Brimelow, *Alien Nation*, pp 249, 254

[lxxxiv] New American Standard Bible, 1977

Afterword:

[lxxxv] John Jay, The Federalist, no. 2 in The Federalist Papers, by Alexander Hamilton, James Madison and John Jay, ed. Clinton Rossiter (1787-88), quoted in Peter Brimelow, *Alien Nation: Common Sense About America's Immigration Disaster,* New York, Random House, 1995p. 210

[lxxxvi] Hamilton, response to Jefferson's message to Congress, 1/12/1802, quoted in Brimelow, *Alien Nation*, 191

[lxxxvii] Frederick Saunders, A Voice To America, New York: Edward Walker, 1855, quoted in A. Cheree Carlson (1989) "The rhetoric of the Know Nothing Party: Nativism as a response to the rhetorical situation," *Southern Communication Journal* 54:4, 364-383

[lxxxviii] "America for Americans", in *The Wide Awake Gift: A Know Nothing Token*, pub. 1866, quoted in Carlson "The rhetoric of the Know Nothing Party"

[lxxxix] Senator Ellison DuRant Smith, Congressional Record, 4/9/1924, 5961-62, quoted in Tom Gjelten, *A Nation of Nations*, New York, Simon and Schuster, 2015

[xc] Quoted in Graham, Otis L., *Unguarded Gates*, Lanham: Rowman and Littlefield, 2004, p. 4

[xci] Abraham Lincoln, Letter to Joshua Speed, August 24, 1855; quoted in Carlson, "The rhetoric of the Know Nothing Party"

[xcii] Emanuel Celler, *You Never Leave Brooklyn*, New York, John Day, 1953

[xciii] Gjelten, *Nation of Nations*, p 98)

[xciv] (Gunnar Myrdal, An American Dilemma: The Negro Problem and Modern Democracy, New York, 1944; quoted in Ronald Takaki, A Different Mirror: A History of Multicultural America, Boston, Little, Brown & Co, 1993)

[xcv] Retrieved from http://www.danielkinouyeinstitute.org/quotes/tags/Patriotism

[xcvi] Annual Msg to the Congress on the State of the Union, 1/8/1964, *Public Papers of the Presidents: Lyndon B Johnson, 1963-1964*, quoted in Gjelten, *Nation of Nations*, 109

[xcvii] Katherine W. Phillips, October 1, 2014, "How Diversity Makes Us Smarter," in Scientific American, retrieved from https://www.scientificamerican.com/article/how-diversity-makes-us-smarter/

[xcviii] Robert E Putnam, *E Pluribus Unum: Diversity and Community in the 21ˢᵗ Century,* Scandinavian Political Studies, vol 30, no 2, 2007, 174, quoted in Gjelten, *Nation of Nations,* p 334

Made in the USA
Middletown, DE
03 September 2022

73096744R00064